# Rainer Werner Fassbinder

# P L A Y S

Edited, Translated, and with an Introduction by
Denis Calandra

**PAJ Publications**
(a division of Performing Arts Journal, Inc.)

New York

*Rainer Werner Fassbinder: Plays* is published by PAJ Publications, P. O. Box 532, Village Station, New York, NY 10014. Distributed to the trade by Consortium Book Sales and Distribution: www.cbsd.com

Publisher of PAJ Publications: Bonnie Marranca

Publication of this book has been made possible in part by funds received from the National Endowment for the Arts, Washington, D.C., a federal agency, and the New York State Council on the Arts.

LIBRARY OF CONGRESS CATALOGING-IN-PUBLICATION DATA

Rainer Werner Fassbinder: Plays
Library of Congress Card Catalog No.: 85-60186
ISBN: 0-933826-81-8 (cloth)
ISBN: 0-933826-82-6 (paper)

ISBN: 978-0-933826-82-3 (13-digit number)

*For Jean*

# Acknowledgments

I would like to thank the library staff of the University of South Florida and Donna Pontonero of the theatre departmental staff for help on the Fassbinder project. Betty Lichtenberg's secretarial and research assistance also deserves special credit. Susan Doepner was of great help on the first draft of *Blut am Hals der Katze*. For sharp critiques of all the translations I would like to thank especially Georg Kleine. Thanks are also due Adam Parfrey for his patient and creative editorial assistance. I am grateful to Hermann Wündrich of Verlag der Autoren for clarifying dozens of points and for much useful information.

D. C.

# Contents

# The Antiteater of R. W. Fassbinder

## Denis Calandra

Rainer Werner Fassbinder began his work in the theatre in the late sixties, as a twenty-two-year-old. He acted, directed, (loosely) adapted classics by Büchner, Goethe, Sophocles, Goldoni and others, wrote several of his own plays, and in a few years emerged as the leader of a group of performers who would work with him, intensively at first, then off and on until his death in 1982. The opposition spirit of the era, however vaguely understood, pervaded the activities of the most diverse independent German theatres. Fassbinder joined the Action-Theater, some of whose members then formed what was to become "his" antiteater: the groups' names tell a story in themselves. The title of one of Handke's earliest plays, *Offending the Audience*, is another typical indicator. Fassbinder's place in the line of haters of traditional theatre can be seen in his affinity with early Brecht. He played the title role in Volker Schlöndorff's 1969 TV film of *Baal*; the focus on raw power-struggles in city-jungles which eat up their inhabitants connects the young anarchic Brecht with his fellow Bavarian and self-advertised enfant-terrible, Fassbinder. (Responding to Fassbinder's death, Werner Herzog said he wasn't German at all, but a "wild" Bavarian.) Fassbinder also shared in and encouraged the revival of the realistic and folk play tradition associated with Odön von Horváth, and especially Marieluise Fleisser. Besides adapting and directing Fleisser's work, his own *Katzelmacher*, dedicated to her, shares the attention to crippling small town mentality as embedded in working class and lower middle class ordinary speech.

Regardless of material, the antiteater productions came to be greeted with certain expectations. Their style apparently had less to do with particular methods, or sets of exercises, than it did with an atmosphere largely created by the theatre's leader. In his book *Fassbinder: Film Maker*, Ronald Hayman writes that Fassbinder "was a creative artist in the plural: the shared work that gave him insight into his own experience gave them excited insight into theirs." German theatre critic Peter Iden described the feel of an antiteater performance in these terms:

> A great spontaneity in the playing, the tendency to explain the choice of material as arbitrary; random and irrational factors in the handling of the productions . . . but also vehemently passionate acting, and a light, nonchalant kind of aggressiveness.[1]

Fassbinder's choice of an English title for *Pre-Paradise Sorry Now* places it firmly in its era. It was anti-Living Theatre, the direct reference being to the American group's *Paradise Now*. Though Action-Theater and anti-teater seemed to share, theoretically at least, the ethos of collective creation and a vague yearning for anarchic freedom, Fassbinder's play clearly mocks the idea of ever achieving paradise, now *or* later. The central plot material has to do with an actual case, the famous English moors murders, committed by Ian Brady and Myra Hindley. Brady teaches Hindley to "enjoy submission"; together they prepare for *their* future paradise, when "inferior creatures" will learn from the master race that "death means happiness." Intercut with this material are a series of neo-realist vignettes demonstrating "the fascistoid underpinnings of everyday life," and a series of Christian liturgical passages which reveal their basis in cannibalism. The vignettes cover familiar Fassbinder territory: whores and pimps; landlords and tenants; pupils and teachers; children and parents—all to do with oppression. The play has an interesting formal structure, in that Fassbinder designated only the Brady/Hindley story to proceed in a set order. The rest can be, and has been, arranged however the production team sees fit. The result is that the beginning, middle and end of the Brady/Hindley plot drives towards a murderous conclusion propelled by the other two structures in the play.

The other Fassbinder play based on a historical event is *Bremen Freedom*, which was written specifically for that city. The play's subject matter is in the realist tradition: a nineteenth century woman systematically eliminates the men and women who would keep her in her proper place. Her own demise is as expected as the repetition of the song she sings with each murder: "World farewell! of thee I'm tired . . ." At the end she murders her friend Luisa in order to save her "from the kind of life you're having to lead." Even in this most conventional play, a black comedy, preserved on film as Fassbinder directed it, hopelessness outruns freedom. The round-dance of courtships and cheerful murders by which Geesche ("in the end a businesswoman") apparently rids herself of her oppressors, leads only to isolation and execution, rather than to liberation. In the film, Margit Carstensen's role as Geesche makes her seem as though she had just stepped off the last pages of *Miss Julie*, on the way to *her* inevitable suicide, into Fassbinder's landscape. Her apparent somnambulism declares her to be in the grip of some unseen force. (Fassbinder had long wanted to, and while with Frankfurt's Theater Am Turm [TAT] eventually did, play the part of Jean in Strindberg's play.)

So it is for the majority of Fassbinder's dramatic characters, whether it be embodied in the routine violence perpetrated on Jorgos the Greek laborer in *Katzelmacher* or the serial misery demonstrated in the generations of daughters and lovers in *The Bitter Tears of Petra von Kant*. In *Petra*, and later in the film *Querelle*, however, though the outcome is the same as for heterosexual characters, his treatment of homosexual relations, as a given, without any need of rationalization, marks an important feature of his work. Even here, though, there has been some dispute over the net result of the picture of homosexuality he paints.[2]

The program cover for the 1971 antiteater production of *Blood On the Cat's Neck* features a picture of Fassbinder, seated, wearing an ascot to cover his throat. On his lap sits an oversize white kitten, obviously a cut-out, spewing liquid from its mouth. The Nuremberg subtitle for the play, in French, is "Marilyn Monroe vs. the Vampires." Who exactly the Kitty is, and who is sucking whose blood isn't worth worrying about, though the vampire motif carries over into the play. (The joke could easily have been an in-group reference to Fassbinder's relationship with his actors. Considerable space is given in the various published memoirs to the ways in which Fassbinder and his group "fed" and "fed on" each other.)

Phoebe Zeitgeist, well known from the cartoon strip, is the main character who eventually goes for everyone's jugular. Sent from a foreign planet to study human democracy, she has trouble interacting, because although she has learned the words, she never really seems to understand human language. She listens to familiar Fassbinder monologues about betrayal, about brutality of loved ones and children, worker exploitation *etc.*; then she witnesses a series of vignettes in the style of *Pre-Paradise Sorry Now* and picks up isolated gestures and phrases. The comedy ensues when she utters the phrases without knowing the right context, or combines them with the wrong gestures. The rest of the characters, as she sinks her teeth into them one by one, descend into a state of torpor. The joke that she may have understood humanity only too well, is capped with her last lines, an extended quotation from Immanuel Kant on the faculty of human understanding.

The alienation is absolute. In his preliminary notes for a film he never made, *Cocaine*, Fassbinder said he wanted to allow his audience, without any help from him, to make the choice between a short, fulfilled life, or a longer existence, which would for the most part be "alienated" and lived outside a "fully conscious" state.[3] His plays, like the films, are about varieties of alienation, and there seem to be no ways out for him short of the desperate, "fulfilling" gestures. The images Fassbinder created for the stage, and in films, linger as grotesque and brutal, possessing a strange, improbable truth.

## Fassbinder's Last Play: Garbage, The City and Death

Fassbinder's major efforts at writing for the theatre ended during the 1974-75 season when he left his position as artistic director of Frankfurt's Theater am Turm in the storm of controversy which surrounded his last play, *Garbage, The City and Death*.[4] As Fassbinder told the story, a group of actors had been trying to put together material on the topic of property speculation and political corruption in Frankfurt. When they foundered, he stepped in to shape the script, which owes some of its features to Gerhard Zwerenz's 1973 novel, *The Earth is Uninhabitable—Like the Moon*.[5] "The play openly displays its weaknesses," Fassbinder wrote, adding that he didn't want "to hide behind any protective form." He felt a writer must be able to explore his themes using methods which are "dangerous, and maybe leave him open to attack." The city of Frankfurt halted production plans before rehearsals could even start, and eventually Suhrkamp, which had published the play, withdrew it from print. These actions were largely due to pressure exerted by the Jewish community, who accused Fassbinder of anti-semitism.

Joachim Fest writing in the *Frankfurter Allgemiene Zeitung* was especially critical: the play was an example of "left-wing fascism"; the writer was using anti-semitism as a "radical chic tactic"; "the leftists" needed a new "suggestive enemy-figure" and found him in Fassbinder's real-estate speculator, The Rich Jew (called Abraham in the Zwerenz novel). Fassbinder, not exactly endeared to the German left, seemed shocked by the extent of the reaction, pointing out the consistent defense of minorities in his other work, and explaining that his Rich Jew, besides being the only one who can feel and express love in the play, is simply doing business, making use of conditions which he did not create. According to Fassbinder, it was a repetition, on a different plane, of developments in the eighteenth century when Jews were the only ones who could be involved in the money market. The Rich Jew, the only main character in the play without a proper name, does act unscrupulously, exploiting bad conscience among other things to make a profit.

There are definite anti-semitic remarks and speeches by characters in the play. Dr. E. L. Ehrlich of B'nai B'rith objected to the central focus Fassbinder gave The Rich Jew, when corrupt business practice is not limited to any single group in Frankfurt. His letter to Suhrkamp dismissed the script as "a botched piece of work," an example of "political pornography," in which "a disgusting anti-semitic tirade in the mouth of a fascist [is] found among similar anti-semitic remarks spread through the play." When playwright Heiner Müller responded to the affair several years later he suggested thematic reasons for the play's focus: "Fassbinder's *Garbage, The City and Death* uses a victim's revenge to describe the devastation of a city in huge, harsh images. The city is Frankfurt. The means of revenge is real estate speculation and its consequences. The perversion of human relationships through their commodity character demonstrates a Biblical piece of wisdom: that the first fratricide, Cain, was also the first to establish a city. Fassbinder said it all in 1976 when he responded in *Theater Heute* to accusations of anti-semitism in the play: 'There are anti-semites in this play. But then they exist in other places too—in Frankfurt for instance.' "

The affair didn't die with Fassbinder. In August, 1984, Frankfurt officials once again stopped a production, this one planned to take place in a subway station under construction near the Old Opera House, the management of which had already contracted a director and a company of actors. Fassbinder's former wife, Ingrid Caven, was one of those engaged. The general manager of the Old Opera House was fired as a result of the controversy. With all the references to "B-level," or "subway people," in *Garbage, The City and Death*—those who literally and metaphorically live a secondary, underground existence in Frankfurt—the planned setting couldn't have been more appropriate. Even the association with opera made sense, for in his play Fassbinder had concocted an "entertainment" porridge out of kitschy music, ballads, sleazy drag routines, fifties rock and roll, and numbers from the great romantic tradition—duets from *La Traviata*, the *Liebestod*, etc. Petty rivalries between the municipal theatre system, originally set to act as co-producer, and the recently renovated Old Opera House, added fuel to the controversy.

However, anti-semitism on the one hand, and imputed infringement of the Bundesrepublik's guarantee (under the *Grundgesetz*, or Basic Law) of free expression on the other, were the chief issues. They are *always* the underlying issues, and rumors of behind the scenes financial pressures to keep the play from opening only intensified the situation. The Nazis had murdered or driven out Frankfurt's substantial Jewish cultural community, and there has been no replacement. This particular absence, in the context of Frankfurt's contribution to the crimes against the Jews, of course limited the debate. *Theater Heute* described the vicious circle that exists, claiming there were Jewish people, among them Israeli citizens, whose dubious business practices reaped for them substantial profits in immediate post-war Frankfurt. Fassbinder had specified that *Garbage, The City and Death* was to be produced in Frankfurt, in a foreign country, or not at all. Bochum and Cologne were both turned down in bids for production rights.

Aspects of the *Garbage* affair were not new to Fassbinder. He was certainly conscious that external circumstances would have an important role in the play's reception, though he couldn't predict what it would be. He could exploit *Garbage*'s event-status in Frankfurt, where the Zwerenz novel had already caused a stir. The entire tenure of Fassbinder at TAT was not a happy one for any of the parties involved. *Garbage* would be a way to rub salt into the eys of his middle class theatre audience as well as gleefully bite the (subsidized) hand that fed him at TAT. Thomas Elseasser's incisive analysis of Fassbinder's immersion in his films simultaneously as works of art, events, speculative commodities, etc. bears quoting in this context:

> Fassbinder's films have been made with "real" money, that is, funds that materialize from the dizzyingly complicated profit-and-loss calculations, the write-offs, deferred and refinancing policies, the ceaseless and now wholly self-evident logic of unlimited speculation. This is the most abstract, intangible form of value and exchange known; its manifestations are "everywhere to be felt, but nowhere to be seen"—a phrase that once referred to the creator of the universe.[6]

Periodically throughout history, as Hannah Arendt has pointed out in *The Origins of Totalitarianism*, the phrase has also been applied to God's enemies, and often enough was skewed to refer to "the Jew in general," the "Jew everywhere and nowhere." Probably the strongest argument against *Garbage* is that it may unwittingly subscribe to the syllogism Jew = Finance = Exploitation: Jew as someone who will put his people's status as victim to work for him in the marketplace. But is that in fact what one would carry away with him from a production of this play, unless one were already predisposed to do so, and would it be the same in New York, say, as in Frankfurt? There are no easy answers.

Portraying The Rich Jew as someone who makes the holocaust turn a quick profit is a consistent, if abhorrent, expression of Fassbinder's view of human relationships. "All evens out in the end," says The Rich Jew in *Garbage*. The Jewish author Jean Améry, who fled Germany in 1938 and was incarcerated in a concentration camp by the Nazis, thought Fassbinder's play "would not be worth bothering with were it not for the figure of The Rich Jew as anti-hero." Fassbinder could be counted on to choose taboo material, and to treat it in an aggressively extreme manner, giving rise to the most disparate responses.

Fassbinder repeatedly explored the idea of power as the determining factor in human relationships. Whether as raw violence or in its subtler forms, parents, lovers, teachers—everyone—seems condemned to exert control, even if they desperately want to do otherwise. Petra von Kant's description of what she wanted with her husband is typical: "We didn't want that stuffy sort of marriage which grinds along in the same old routine. We wanted always to be fully conscious, always to decide for ourselves anew . . . ." That relationship failed, as does her love affair with Karin, because Petra "just wanted to possess her," not really share a love with her.

Fassbinder didn't fail to implicate himself, as is evident in the roles he chose for himself in his films. The most notorious example is Fassbinder as Fassbinder in *Germany in Autumn*, in which he victimizes his lover and brow-beats his mother. In the film version of *Garbage, The City and Death* (*Shadow of Angels* by Daniel Schmid, 1975) Fassbinder played the victimizer/victim, Roma's brutal pimp Franz B. (Raoul in the film), who becomes the *object* of grotesque sexual abuse: the sort of erotics—"Let me discover humility"—Fassbinder further probed in *Querelle*.

Fassbinder's own shameless manipulation of feelings, as if emotional exploitation were the only option, has been well documented. As a drama student, in his earliest contact with theatre, he claims to have paid less attention to learning the craft than to observing the sado-masochism built into the training sessions. In his book on the artist, Ronald Hayman quotes a 1973 remark about Fassbinder's methods with actors: "Rainer solved a great deal simply through terror . . . This tension between the people in the group, it was like a drug."

Fassbinder understood his artistic investment in human misery. In *Garbage*, Roma B. remarks to another prostitute, "Despair—call it by its proper name, that'll raise you capital." In a way, Fassbinder made a career out of despair—selling his own and others' misery in endless variations, operating according to a system he did not create.

## Footnotes

[1]*Fassbinder*, ed. Tony Rayns, British Film Insitute: London, 1974, p. 17. See Ronald Hayman, *Fassbinder: Film Maker*, Simon and Schuster: New York, 1984, especially Chapter 2, "The Group and The Team," for an account in English of Fassbinder's work in different German theatres.

[2]See Dyer, "Reading Fassbinder's Sexual Politics," in Rayns, ed., *Fassbinder*, 2nd ed., British Film Institute: London, 1979, pp. 54-64, who suggests Fassbinder's "political effectivity—limited though it is—may be far more important than the films' own political despair. In the end, it is not so much what the films say that matters, but rather what people do with what they say."

[3]*Filmebefreien den Kopf*, ed. Michael Töteberg, Fischer: Frankfurt am Main, 1984, p. 91.

[4]After leaving TAT Fassbinder directed one more play, Clare Booth Luce's *The Women (Frauen in New York)* in Hamburg, 1976; he also used texts from Artaud in the screenplay for his film *Theatre In A Trance* (1981), which includes Pina Bausch, Jerome Savary, Squat Theatre and others.

[5]An interview with Fassbinder and excerpts from the public debate are published with the script in Horst Laube and Brigitte Landes, eds., *Theaterbuch 1*, Carl Hanser Verlag; München, 1978, pp. 275-326; Contributions by Fassbinder and four others (Jean Améry, Karlheinz Braun, Siegfried Unseld, and Gerhard Zwerenz) appear in *Die Zeit*, Nr. 16-9, April, 1976, pp. 33, ff; See also, Joachim Kaiser, "*Gerechtigkeit für Fassbinders Ungerechtigkeit*," *Süddeutsche Zeitung*, March 31, 1976; *Theater Heute*, Nr. 10, August 8, 1984, retells the story, and reports on the 1984 veto of the second attempted Frankfurt

production; Zwerenz tells the story in personal terms in *Der langsame Tod des Rainer Werner Fassbinder*, Knaur: München, 1982. All quotations on the debate are taken from these sources.

[6]"*Lili Marleen*: Fascism and The Film Industry," *October*, No. 21, Summer, 1982, pp. 118-19.

### Productions and Fassbinder premieres
### (Plays directed by Fassbinder unless otherwise specified.)

1967: Büchner's *Leonce and Lena* at the Action-Theatre (collective direction); Bruckner's *The Criminals.*

1968: Marieluise Fleisser's *Pioneers of Ingolstadt* adapted as *For Example Ingolstadt* by Fassbinder (directed with Peer Raben), at the Büchner-Theater; Fassbinder's *Katzelmacher* (directed with Peer Raben); *Axel Caesar Haarmann*, group play, at the antiteater (directed with Peer Raben); Peter Weiss's *Herr Mockinpott* (collective direction)' Jarry's *Ubu Roi*, group adaptation, as *Orgie Ubu* (directed with Jorg Schmitt), both at the antiteater; Goethe's *Iphigenia In Tauris* adapted by Fassbinder at the antiteater; Sophocles' *Ajax* adapted by Fassbinder at the antiteatre; Fassbinder's *The American Soldier* at the antiteater; Gay's *Beggar's Opera* adapted by Fassbinder (directed with Peer Raben), at the antiteater.

1969: Fassbinder's *Pre-Paradise Sorry Now* at the antiteater; Fassbinder's *Anarchy In Bavaria* at the antiteater; Goldoni's *Coffee House* adapted by Fassbinder (directed with Peer Raben); Fassbinder and Harry Baer's *Werewolf* (directed with Peer Raben) both at the antiteater; Lope de Vega's *Fuente Ovejuna* adapted by Fassbinder, directed for the antiteater in Berlin.

1970: Marieluise Fleisser's *Pioneers in Ingolstadt* adapted by Fassbinder (directed by Peer Raben) in Bremen; Fassbinder's *Pre-Paradise Sorry Now* (radio play for Süddeutscher Rundfunk); Fassbinder's *All in White* (radio play for Bayerischer Rundfunk/Hessischer Rundfunk/Süddeutscher Rundfunk).

1971: Fassbinder's *Blood on the Cat's Neck* (directed with Peer Raben) for the antiteater in Nuremberg; Fassbinder's *The Bitter Tears of Petra von Kant* (directed by Peer Raben) for the Landestheater Darmstadt at the Frankfurt Experimenta; Fassbinder's *Bremen Freedom* in Bremen; Goethe's *Iphigenia In Tauris* adapted as radio play by Fassbinder for Westdeutscher Rundfunk.

1972: Ferenc Molnar's *Liliom* in Bochum; Fassbinder's *No One is Evil and No One is Good* (radio play for Bayerischer Rundfunk.)

1973: Heinrich Mann's *Bibi* in Bochum; Ibsen's *Hedda Gabler* at the Volksbühne, Berlin.

1974: Handke's *They Are Dying Out* at the Frankfurt Schauspielhaus; Zola's *Germinal* adapted by Yaak Karsunke at the Theater am Turm, Frankfurt; Chekhov's *Uncle Vanya* at the Theater am Turm.

1976: Clare Booth Luce's *The Women* at the Hamburg Schauspielhaus.

1985: A Munich premiere is planned for Fassbinder's *Tropfen auf heisse Steine*, written in 1968/69.

## Fassbinder: Select Bibliography

### Books

*Antiteater (Katzelmacher, Preparadise sorry now, Die Bettleroper)* Suhrkamp: Frankfurt am Main, 1970.

*Antiteater 2. (Das Kaffeehaus, Bremer Freiheit, Blut am Hals der Katze)*, Suhrkamp: Frankfurt am Main, 1972.

*Stücke 3. (Die bitteren Tränen der Petra von Kant; Das brennende Dorf; Der Müll, die Stadt und der Tod)*, Suhrkamp: Frankfurt am Main, 1976. Withdrawn by the publisher.

*Schatten der Engel, Ein Film von Daniel Schmid nach dem Theaterstück der Müll, die Stadt und der Tod* von Rainer Werner Fassbinder. Zweitausendeins: Frankfurt am Main, 1976.

Hans Günther Pflaum and Rainer Werner Fassbinder, *Das bisschen Realität, das ich brauche. Wie Filme entstehen*. Hanser: München, 1976. Taschenbuchausgabe, DTV: Munchen, 1979.

*Angst essen Seele auf*. G. E. C. Gad: Kopenhagen, 1978.

*Der Film Berlin Alexanderplatz. Ein Arbeitsjournal*. Mit Harry Baer. Zweitausendeins: Frankfurt am Main, 1980.

*Der Müll, die Stadt und der Tod*, Verlag der Autoren: Frankfurt am Main, 1981.

*Hanna Schygulla. Bilder aus Filmen von Rainer Werner Fassbinder*. (Mit einem Bietrag von Fassbinder.)
Schirmer/Morel: Munchen, 1981.

*Die bitteren Tränen der Petra von Kant*, Verlag der Autoren; Frankfurt am Main, 1982.

*Katzelmacher, Preparadise sorry now*, Verlag der Autoren: Frankfurt am Main, 1982.

*Querelle. Filmbuch*, Photographien von Roger Fritz, Herausgegeben von Dieter Schidor und Michael McLernon, Schirmer/Morel: München, 1982.

*Bremer Freiheit, Blut am Hals der Katze*. Verlag der Autoren: Frankfurt am Main, 1983.

*Filme befreien den Kopf*, Herausgegeben von Michael Töteberg, Fischer Taschenbuch Verlag: Frankfurt am Main, 1984.

*Anarchie in Bayern und andere Stücke* [including *Tropfen auf heisse Steine*], Herausgegeben von Michael Töteberg, Verlag der Autoren: Frankfurt am Main, 1985.

### On Fassbinder in English

Calandra, Denis. *New German Dramatists*. Grove Press: New York, 1983.

Corrigan, Timothy. *New German Film*. University of Texas Press: Austin, 1983.

Hayman, Ronald. *Fassbinder: Film Maker*. Simon and Schuster: New York, 1984.

Jansen, Peter W. and Wolfram Schütte, eds., *Fassbinder*, trans., with new article by Ruth McCormick. Tanam Press: New York, 1981. (Originally published by Carl Hanser: Munich, 1979 [3rd ed.].)

Rayns, Tony, ed., *Fassbinder*. British Film Institute: London, 1974; 2nd ed., 1979.

"Rainer Werner Fassbinder Special Issue." *October* (No. 21). MIT Press: Cambridge, Mass., 1982.

Sandford, John. *The New German Cinema*. Barnes and Noble: Totowa, NewJersey, 1980.

## On Fassbinder in German

Baer, Harry. *Schlafen kann ich, wenn ich tot bin. Das atemlose Leben des Rainer Werner Fassbinder.* Kiepenheuer und Witsch: Köln, 1982.

Eckhardt, Bernd. *Rainer Werner Fassbinder.* Heyne: München, 1982.

Jansen, Peter W. and Wolfram Schütte, eds., *Fassbinder*, Carl Hanser: München, 1974, 1979.

Laube, Horst and Brigitte Landes. *Theaterbuch 1.* Carl Hanser: München, 1978.

Limmer, Wolfgang. *Rainer Werner Fassbinder Filmemacher.* Rowohlt: Reinbeck, 1981.

Raab, Kurt und Karsten Peters. *Die Sehnsucht des Rainer Werner Fassbinder.* C. Bertelsmann: München, 1982.

Schidor. Dieter. *Rainer Werner Fassbinder dreht Querelle.* [With contributions by Christian Enzensberger and Wolf Wondratschek]. Heyne: München, 1982.

Zwerenz, Gerhard. *Der langsame Tod des Rainer Werner Fassbinder.* Knaur: München, 1982.

# The Bitter Tears
# of
# Petra von Kant

CHARACTERS:

Petra von Kant
Valerie von Kant, her mother
Gabriele von Kant, her daughter
Sidonie von Grasenabb, her friend
Karin Thimm, her lover
Marlene, her personal secretary

# ACT ONE

*Marlene draws the curtain. Loudly.*

PETRA: Marlene! Can you not be more sensitive! My head is so . . . heavy. Like lead. The telephone. Quick! (*Marlene gives her the telephone, Petra dials.*) Hello? Frau von Kant please. Of course I'll wait. Squeeze me some oranges. I'm dying of thirst! Mama! I couldn't get back to you yesterday, mama. Work. You know how it is. No. I've been up for ages. Really. Not a minute to relax. But I suppose I should be thankful for that. Where are you going? Mama? Oh, I'm so happy for you mother. Miami is absolutely delightful. Honest, absolutely delightful. And the people. Fabulous social life. Simply fabulous. Six months!? Oh, mama. I'm speechless. Six months. God how I envy you. Six months in Miami. That wouldn't do me a bit of harm either. (*Marlene brings the juice. Petra covers the mouthpiece.*) Thanks. Get started with the drawing. The sketches are in the file drawer. Yes mama? How's that? Mama, of course I've been listening to you, but there's some problem with the connection. I'm sorry. Don't be offended. Really, it was just some interference in the line. I'm not lying! That is insulting, mother. Okay, I'm listening to you mama. Yes, I understand. Of course. Yes. How much do you need, then? Eight thousand? That's a lot of money. Wait a second. (*She covers the mouthpiece.*) What should I do? (*Marlene shrugs her shoulders.*) You're never any help either, are you?! Mama! Alright, I can lend you five thousand. Right now anything more is out of the question. But you know about all my expenses, and Gabriele on top of that. Perhaps you can try to get the rest from Tatjana or . . . yes, mama. 'Til later. Ciao. (*She stands up and lights a cigarette.*) Marlene. You have to write a letter, quick. To Joseph

Mankewitz. The address is in the file. (*Marlene puts paper in the typewriter.*) Dear Mankewitz, dear friend, comma, unfortunately it will be impossible for me to make the payment. Period. There are circumstances in this vale of tears, dot, dot, dot. But who am I telling this to, question mark. Hoping you will understand, I remain, in friendship, yours, Petra von Kant. I'll sign right away. Come here. (*Marlene lets Petra sign.*) Take care of it, and hurry.

(*Marlene goes. Petra gets up and puts on a Platters record. When it is half played Marlene returns. Petra dances to the music; etc.*)

PETRA: Alright, get on with it, the drawing has to be finished by noon. Any mail? (*Marlene brings the mail.*) Karstadt? (*She opens the lettter.*) I'm to do a collection for Karstadt! Marlene, did you hear that? What an opportunity! (*She goes to the telephone, dials.*) Karstadt? Herr Müller-Freienfels please. My name is Petra von Kant. Thank you. This is Petra von Kant. Yes, I have . . . yes. But this week is tight. Did you say Friday? Hang on. Yes, Friday I can make it. What time? Three? Okay. Three o'clock. 'Til then. Ciao. (*She hangs up.*) Bastards! You remember three years ago when I had to grovel to get them to look at my first collection? Times have indeed changed. What gorgeously submissive tones from the good man! When you think of it . . . (*Doorbell rings.*) What now for God's sake? Who . . .? (*Marlene shrugs her shoulders.*) Who cares! Let them in. (*Marlene goes out. Petra dials a number.*) Ten thirty. Doesn't matter.

(*Marlene and Sidonie von Grasenabb enter.*)

SIDONIE: Darling!
PETRA: Sidonie! Dearest!
SIDONIE: Petra! (*They embrace.*)
PETRA: My God, how long . . .
SIDONIE: Three years darling. Three years. How time flies. And you still look as good as ever. Terribly good. It's a wonder how you do it.
PETRA: You have me beat in each and every category, my dear good friend: looks, youth, all of them.
SIDONIE: And Frank? (*Petra shakes her head.*) I read about the two of you. In Australia! Think of it. And at once I said to Lester, I said, poor Petra now she's paying the price. All of us repeatedly warned you about that man.
PETRA: Experience, Sidonie. We all have to live our own lives. I'm glad to have gone through it just the way it was. They can't take your experience away from you. Quite the contrary. It makes you grow.
SIDONIE: I don't know Petra. If you can see how things are going to turn out right from the start, can the experience really be worth very much?
PETRA: Marlene, make some coffee. Or would you prefer tea?

SIDONIE: Coffee's just fine.

PETRA: Have you had breakfast?

SIDONIE: Yes, thank you. I flew in this morning from Frankfurt. I couldn't get you off my mind, how you were bearing up, whether you were suffering . . .

PETRA: Come now, Sidonie. People mature. In the old days . . . back then I was different, sure. I'd have had no idea where to turn. The shame of it alone. I believed so firmly in the man's goodness. But it's true, you know, in marriage the flawed sides of our characters take over.

SIDONIE: I'm not so sure. With Lester . . .

PETRA: I'm sorry but with all your trips you've never had the time to really get to know one another. You know for a fact it was different with Frank and me: together day and night with hardly a break. I was nearly always afraid, insecure. In those circumstances you can get to know what another person is made of . . . I apologize. I didn't want to become bitter, but there really could have been possibilities for that man and me. It simply wasn't in the cards.

SIDONIE: You still dream about it?

PETRA: No, Sidonie. There's no denying I still brood over the prospects there were for the two of us. Believe me it's sad when you realize that what's irritating in a relationship far outweighs the beautiful things you experience.

SIDONIE: Did you quarrel, or . . . ?

PETRA: Quarrel? Not in the literal sense. There was something frigid in the air sometimes, you know how you notice . . . For instance, you're together with another person, in your car or in a room, and you want to say something but you are afraid. You'd like to be tender, but again you grow frightened. You're frightened of defeat, of being the weaker one. That's the horrible point at which you know there's no giving in.

SIDONIE: I guess I understand what you mean. Not very clearly, but . . .

PETRA: I know what you are going to say. It would be wiser to give in, for instance. Or . . . No, Sidonie, once a relationship is stuck fast in its own sweet tar pit, you show me the person who can pull it out again.

SIDONIE: It can't have been like this for three years.

PETRA: Of course not. There were moments, they were so fine that . . . you know when you forget everything, everything. Even the old problems, and think you could find a new basis for . . . oh it was a mess.

SIDONIE: You poor dear thing.

PETRA: Sidonie, it's very easy to feel pity; understanding's a lot harder. If you understand someone, you shouldn't pity them. You can change them. You should feel pity only where you don't understand.

SIDONIE: I can see the whole affair has hardened you. Sad, but I've always been suspicious of hard women.

PETRA: I only seem hard because I'm using my brain. You don't seem accustomed to the idea that women think. Poor baby.

SIDONIE: Petra! Please!

PETRA: I'm sorry. I didn't mean to offend you. I only want you to hear what I'm telling you, really hear it, and not to use any preconceived notions to judge what I'm saying before I've even finished formulating my thoughts.

SIDONIE: Certainly. I can understand your bitterness. Was *he* the one who . . . filed for divorce?

PETRA: No, I did.

SIDONIE: Not him?! You . . . Christ!

PETRA: That surprises you, huh? Poor little Petra who'd never leave the man, who seemed hopelessly in love, slavishly so, she filed for divorce. How dreadful, right?

SIDONIE: Did he . . .

PETRA: No, he didn't cheat. To start with, infidelity couldn't warrant separation as far as I'm concerned. The relationship in my opinion was quite healthy. We both valued a good time. Being faithful wasn't important, at least being faithful out of a sense of duty. In that regard we were true to each other. No, there were different grounds for it not working. Naturally, when things are going awry, hatred surfaces, and repulsion. It has nothing to do with what was going on around us, or between us and other people, or . . . (*Marlene enters and serves coffee.*) Thank you.

SIDONIE: Thank you.

PETRA: Now please get on with the drawing. We're pressed for time. (*Marlene draws.*)

SIDONIE: Can we . . .?

PETRA: Marlene? Marlene's been with me for three years. She hears everything, sees everything, knows everything. Don't worry about Marlene.

SIDONIE: Alright, let's continue. Then what was it that alienated you from one another, troubled you so?

PETRA: Oh, Sidonie!

SIDONIE: Look, Petra, Lester and I went through a period when it seemed like it was over. Like we'd just had enough, even felt a mutual . . . disgust. Well . . . you have to be shrewd, you know, understanding, and brimming with humility. A woman's wiles exercised in the correct manner . . .

PETRA: I didn't want to *exercise* any *wiles*, Sidonie, and definitely not the sort designated "for women only." I wanted to forgo all conjuring tricks.

SIDONIE: Tricks, Petra? I . . .

PETRA: Yes! They're tricks. Cheap ones at that. And all they really do is put you in bondage. When I hear words like humility I . . .

SIDONIE: Don't make fun, Petra. Please don't make fun. Lester and I are happy now, really! The humility paid off. He thinks he controls me and I don't disillusion him. In the end, really, I get my own way.

PETRA: Darling, look, I understand what you're saying. Maybe it's just right, too, for you and Lester. Perhaps this kind of control is exactly what you need. Yet . . . you know, Frank and I, we had to have a rare and fine kind of love. And fine for us meant always to know exactly what was going on inside yourself, and inside your partner. We didn't want that stuffy sort of marriage which grinds along in the same old routine. We wanted to be fully conscious, always to decide for ourselves anew, always . . . free.

SIDONIE: Petra, I don't know why you make things difficult when they can be so simple. The "routines" are there, for example, for you to make use of. If you need to find something new even when the old will do, well, go ahead.

PETRA: We wanted to be happy together. Do you understand that: together. There is no proven formula.

SIDONIE: Then what happened to cause the disgust? When there was so much clarity, so much understanding?

PETRA: Success, for one thing. Success, which I had and which Frank was yearning for, and which he actually needed. That's how it started. So simple.

SIDONIE: Yes. I'm sorry but success is no reason to . . .

PETRA: Men! And their vanity. My God, Sidonie. He wanted to provide for me, pamper me. Sure, he took himself quite seriously, and of course he conceded me my own opinions. Nevertheless, he wanted me kept. And so, in this roundabout way and all on its own, oppression made itself felt. You know how it goes—"I hear what you are saying, I understand, but . . .who earns the money, breaks his back?" What a double standard! Dearest Sidonie! In the early days it went like this: "What you earn, my little girl, we'll put in a special bank account and later on the time will be right to spend it; maybe a little house or a sports car or something." I nodded, agreed, because . . . he was so loving, Sidonie, and the love he bathed us in truly overwhelmed me with joy . . . took my breath away. When he began to go under, you know, at the start it was almost laughable to watch, how his stupid pride was hurt, and to be quite honest I enjoyed it, especially since I really thought he was aware how absurd his behavior was. He wasn't aware. Then later when I tried to explain, to tell him that for me there was no difference at all if a man was "on top" or not, it was already too late. As soon as the subject was raised, Sidonie, there was a wall, a wall. Then bit by bit all honesty between us began to die. I felt I had been mistaken about him, about myself, and then I ended it. Stopped loving him. The last six months were horrible, believe me, horrible! Of course he knew it was finished, or at least suspected as much. He wouldn't tolerate it, not him. He wasn't too clever. He tried to hang on to me, at least in bed. But the disgust came with that part. He tried technique, then force. I let him mount me. Endured it. But . . . he seemed so filthy to me.

SIDONIE: Petra!

PETRA: He stank. He smelled like a man. Just the way men stink. And what used to arouse me . . . now made me want to vomit, to cry. The way he humped me.

SIDONIE: Petra, Petra. Don't.

PETRA: Now you have to hear the story out. He had me the way a bull takes his cow. Not a glimmer of respect, no concern for his woman's pleasure. Sidonie, the suffering . . . suffering you couldn't dream of. Sometimes when I . . . oh the shame! The shame. I felt ashamed. He thought I was squealing in pleasure, in love, thankful. He was so stupid, so stupid. Men are so stupid.

SIDONIE: You poor, poor thing. How you've suffered.

PETRA: I don't need your sympathy. He . . . he could have used mine. Understanding, kindness or sympathy, just when nothing else is possible. I didn't feel anything for him any more. On the contrary, it got worse. When we ate together his chewing split my eardrums, the slurping—I couldn't stand it. The way he cut his meat, ate vegetables, or the way he held a cigarette, a whisky glass. It all seemed so ridiculous to me, so . . . affected. I was ashamed for him because I thought everyone who saw him must feel the same as I did. Of course it was panic, Sidonie, hysteria. There was nothing to salvage. Gone. Finished. Done with. (*Pause.*) I am ashamed.

SIDONIE: You needn't be. You needn't be ashamed. You tried to learn from it. Tried to grasp . . . I . . .

PETRA: I guess people are made so as to need other people, yet . . . they haven't learned how to be together. (*Doorbell rings.*) Marlene!

(*Marlene gets up, exits.*)

SIDONIE: That must be Karin.

PETRA: Karin?

SIDONIE: A charming young lady. I met her on the ship from Sydney to Southampton. She wants to make a life for herself in Germany.

(*Marlene enters with Karin.*)

SIDONIE: Karin?

KARIN: Hello.

SIDONIE: This is Petra, the Petra von Kant I was telling you so much about.

KARIN: Pleased to meet you.

PETRA: Pleased to meet you. Do sit down. I apologize for the mess. Things are a bit chaotic.

KARIN: No problem.

PETRA: Tea? Or cognac?

KARIN: Cognac, yes please.

PETRA: Marlene! Cognac. You, Sidonie?

SIDONIE: Come now, in the morning? No, thank you.

KARIN: Funny, I pictured you to be a lot older, more . . . distinguished. Do people use that word?

PETRA: Yes, people do. But why older?

KARIN: Success and fame. I don't know . . . it somehow goes with age.

SIDONIE: Exceptions prove the rule.

(*Marlene brings two cognac glasses, pours.*)

PETRA: Here's to you.

KARIN: And you.

SIDONIE: Well, we should be moving on, Karin. Petra! I'll call you when I get the chance. I'll be here longer this trip. Ciao.

PETRA: You do that Sidonie. Be good. Bye.

KARIN: Bye. (*Sidonie is already out. Marlene has gone ahead.*)

PETRA: Er, ummm . . .

KARIN: (*Turns.*) Yes?

PETRA: You have a nice figure. You could get somewhere. Get in touch if you have a mind to.

KARIN: With pleasure.

PETRA: What about tomorrow? Tomorrow evening. Around eight.

SIDONIE: Karin!

KARIN: I'm coming. 'Til tomorrow.

PETRA: 'Til tomorrow.

(*Karin leaves. Petra steps up to the easel and inspects Marlene's drawing. Marlene enters.*)

PETRA: You changed the sleeves? Well . . . that's not bad. It's better that way.

# ACT TWO

*Bright, but it is evening. Petra runs across the stage like a scared chicken, dressing herself. Puts herself in order. Marlene helps her with the buttons, etc., intermittently types. Doorbell rings.*

PETRA: Marlene! The doorbell, Marlene. I'm not nearly ready. Open up, I'll be right there.

*(Both exit. After a minute Marlene enters with Karin, shows her to a seat, then returns to her desk. Karin gets up, walks to the mirror and has a long look at herself. Petra enters.)*

PETRA: Karin! How pleasant.
KARIN: *(Slowly turning around.)* Good evening, Frau von Kant.
PETRA: *(Goes up to her as if to embrace her, but stops short.)* Let's sit down. I've prepared a few trifles. Marlene! The food tray! *(Marlene leaves.)* So here you are.
KARIN: Yes, here I am. *(They both laugh.)*
PETRA: Are you enjoying Germany?
KARIN: Well I've only been away five years. Yes, I like it. Hasn't changed much.
PETRA: Nothing changes much here. In Germany things are the way they are. Nothing you can do about it. Tell me about yourself.
KARIN: Me? There's not much to tell.
PETRA: Sure there is. What you think, or dream about.
KARIN: Very little. I'd like to find a place for myself in the world. Is that asking too much?

PETRA: No, quite the contrary, Karin, quite the contrary. That's what it is to be alive, to struggle to establish a place for yourself.

KARIN: And . . . is it necessary to . . . fight for it?

PETRA: Definitely. Even I had to fight, and hard, let me tell you. That's just the way it is.

KARIN: I don't know. I've always considered myself too lazy for any kind of struggle.

PETRA: Too lazy?

KARIN: Yes. You see I mostly enjoy lying in bed, reading magazines, novels, that sort of thing. That's . . .

PETRA: Perhaps you haven't had the right incentive yet, in your life. You're still quite young.

KARIN: Twenty-three.

PETRA: Exactly. There's still a lot ahead of you at that age. Good and bad, beautiful and hideous. After all, life's just getting started at twenty-three.

KARIN: Yeah?

PETRA: Yes. Or don't you agree?

KARIN: Oh God, I've already done a few things. I'm married, and . . .

PETRA: You are . . . Oh, is that so?

KARIN: Yes. My husband stayed behind in Australia. We had . . . Oh, things aren't so very simple.

PETRA: No. Nothing is simple. Nothing at all. A person has to exercise humility.

KARIN: Humility?

PETRA: Yes, you see each of us has a particular theory of the world. Mine is that if a person is to bear those things he truly understands he must be humble.I stand in humility before my work for example, and before the money it provides me. And before many things much more powerful than I am.

KARIN: "Humility" is such a comical word. It reminds me of—genuflection and praying. I don't know, I . . .

PETRA: It's possible these . . . ideas . . . aren't meant for young people. I wouldn't have responded any differently at your age.

(Marlene brings in a tray and places it on the table in front of them.)

PETRA: Thank you. Help yourself. (Marlene returns to work at her desk.) But do you think it would be fun to work as a model, for instance?

KARIN: I don't know the business, or what I'd, sort of, be getting into, but in principle—why not?

PETRA: Wonderful. We'll have to sit down soon and iron out the details. Of course you can't just dive in and presto know it all. You'd have to be prepared to learn.

KARIN: I want to learn. No question. I'm not asking for it on a platter.

PETRA: Of course, I can make it easier for you. Later on when you know your way around you won't have to worry about getting a job.

KARIN: Thank you.

PETRA: At the start you might have problems, I mean money problems. While you are taking courses you won't be making any money.

KARIN: Probably. I . . .

PETRA: I will help you. Consider that an offer. There won't be any problem there.

KARIN: Yes. That's very kind of you.

PETRA: You know what's nice about this profession? You are on the move a lot. I love foreign capitals at night. Do you like to travel?

KARIN: Depends. Yeah, I guess so.

PETRA: It can be great. Underway a lot, seeing, experiencing new things. Foreign cities, music. Do you like art?

KARIN: Art? I don't know.

PETRA: Theatre, concerts, good films? Hmmm?

KARIN: Sure. I like to go to the movies. Love stories, yeah. Tearjerkers. Real nice.

PETRA: (*Dubious.*) Of course. We can study together. There's a lot we can do. You know I was lucky when it came to parents. At an early age I was introduced to the finer things in life. What were your parents? . . . I mean what did they do for a living?

KARIN: My father was a machine worker.

PETRA: Really? Very interesting.

KARIN: Yeah. Wasn't so great. Work, not much fun. That's how it is. They didn't have a lot of excitement in their lives. Tiny apartment, three kids, constant shouting.

PETRA: But your parents, I mean they must have taken good care of you as a child.

KARIN: "Taken care of us?" We were there, and we were a pain. At least most of the time.

PETRA: Poor thing. It must have been horrible.

KARIN: Nah! They meant well, both of them. Besides, they nearly always left us alone. I think that's better than having parents who butt into everything. You know, into what you're thinking and all.

PETRA: Nevertheless, to simply leave children to their own devices. I don't know. I have a daughter. Naturally I can't always be looking after her, but I know that she is definitely at one of the very best boarding schools. Knowing that puts me at ease, believe me. I loved school. You?

KARIN: I . . . no. No, I guess not. I still remember I was happy when it was over. Although I think I was pretty good in school.

PETRA: You certainly are very intelligent.

KARIN: Intelligent, yeah, that I suppose. But I wasn't much interested in studying then. Subjects I liked, that was okay. Yeah.

PETRA: That's how it was with me. I was always tops in things that interested me. Oddly enough back then I had a real penchant for mathematics.

KARIN: Not me. I was always lousy in arithmetic. Well, as a beginner I was okay, but later when we got to using letters of the alphabet I didn't know what was going on.

PETRA: Strange. Algebra always gave me an incredible charge, incredible!

KARIN: Algebra, that was it. No, not for me. I could never work out why such and such a number got such and such a letter, know what I mean? It's still a mystery.

PETRA: Well it's not so important anyway. There are more pressing things in the world.

KARIN: Gym was cool. And track in spring semester. Or the games, sort of, like field hockey and elimination. I never cared for those sorts of apparatuses though, like the parallel bars or the horizontals. Spring semester I got "A's," and in the fall, "C's."

PETRA: Is that so? No, I actually preferred working on the apparatus. That takes —discipline. The kind of word hated by today's young people.

KARIN: I don't know, discipline's okay by me, long as you have fun too. But if it's just sort of discipline, or sort of heavy-pressure, I don't like that.

PETRA: Funny, but—well for instance I need motivation to do something. If I need money for example, or to make good on a promise. Your way . . . without any external pressure . . . sometimes I'd really be in the pits.

KARIN: Yeah, I guess I can understand that, but I still think it's better without the pressure. My father for example. Every Sunday he took us on a bike trip. The whole family pedaling along. First him, then mother, then the three girls, ranked according to age. And did he ever speed! After all he was a man. We were wiped out when we got home at night. But him: he was fresh as a daisy. And then he'd argue with mama, over something stupid. Oh well. We had no choice. We had to go. Each and every time. I'd have been happy to bike along at my own pace, but the way it was I never had any fun. Never. Although right now the whole thing seems real funny. Imagine it: a father, mother and three daughters on bicycles.

PETRA: It is funny. But of course what your father did was brutal. That's still not the pressure I'm talking about. I mean the kind of pressure one accepts, needs, even yearns for. In order to accomplish something, as I see it. You have to get somewhere in life. How are your parents doing now?

KARIN: My father and mother are dead.

PETRA: I'm sorry. Both.

KARIN: First my father killed my mother, then he hung himself.

PETRA: No! How horrible!

KARIN: See the way you're looking at me? Completely different now. Exactly

like the rest of them. First you think I'm okay, then you find out my story,
and bye bye.

PETRA: No, Karin, no. I feel . . . quite tender toward you, I . . . now that I know
your history I feel even more . . . I must do right by you. Let us be the
closest, dearest of friends. What do you say?

KARIN: Sure. Let's.

PETRA: Marlene! Bring us a glass of champagne. (*Marlene exits.*) She's a good
girl. Does all my work. But do tell me how it all happened . . .

KARIN: Happened with my parents? It was very simple. Didn't you read about it
in the newspapers, the whole story?

PETRA: No, no, I don't remember.

KARIN: Papa drank a lot and . . . no, that's not the way it goes, because . . .
one day on the job they told papa, "Herr Thimm, we are a forward looking
firm," something like that, "and there's no room for people your age any
longer." I'm not sure exactly how it went because I wasn't there, but that's
close. He lost control, broke down crying, and got violent, so the security
guards took him out of the factory. He went to his regular hangout and got
sloshed. What could you expect in a situation like that? And papa drank a
lot anyway. Then he went home, stabbed mama to death, and hung himself.
He thought the world had no use for him or his wife anymore. A simple
story. I left immediately for Australia. But things aren't so rosy there either.
As far as opportunities go. And they sure know how to give you the cold
shoulder if you can't hack it like everyone else.

PETRA: Things are going to be different now, Karin, completely different.
Together we're going to see to it that you make something of your life.

KARIN: That would be wonderful. I was constantly giving up all hope, honest.
With my husband, that was crap too. He made me break my back and kept
saying stuff like he'd make plenty of cash some day. Won't last much longer.
He's been pissing me off long enough.

(*Marlene brings the champagne, opens it, pours two glasses, returns to work.*)

PETRA: Prost. To us. In the hope that we seize our opportunities.

KARIN: Prost.

PETRA: I can already see you on the runway. I will create a collection especially
for you. You'll be a top model. Honest! You are beautiful, Karin. (*She
caresses her, then abruptly gets up and puts on a record: "In My Room" by the
Walker Brothers.*) Do you like this kind of music?

KARIN: Sure, yeah.

PETRA: These records take me back to my youth. They can make me either sad
or happy. It depends. That's when I was with my first husband. What a
glorious love affair. Someone once said beautiful things never last long
—there's truth in that. Pierre was killed in an automobile accident. He had a

passion for driving. Pierre was a . . . he was a beautiful man—but possessed. And . . he thought he was indestructible. He wasn't. By the time our daughter was born he had been dead four months. Fate. It wasn't easy for me. But everything is pre-ordained. One way or the other I'm sure of it. I had to bear it. You know, Karin, people are bad news. In the end they tolerate everything. People are hard and brutal, and one's no different from the next. We just have to accept that. (*They listen as the music concludes.*) Where are you living now?

KARIN: Hotel Rheingold.

PETRA: In a hotel? But that must be expensive?

KARIN: Twenty-seven, with breakfast.

PETRA: Exactly. That doesn't make sense, does it? Move in with me. It's cheaper and . . . besides . . . it's nice here.

KARIN: Huh? I . . .

PETRA: Or don't you want to?

KARIN: Oh, yeah. It'd be great. I'm just afraid that maybe I'll . . . maybe I'll get on your nerves.

PETRA: I know what I'm like Karin. You won't get on my nerves. I know myself. I'm so very often lonely, all on my own. It'll be nice for us.

KARIN: If you think . . . I'd love to. Really. I . . .

PETRA: I love you. I love you, Karin. I love you. Together, we can conquer the world. I'm confused. I want to touch you, and kiss you. I . . . (*She embraces her.*)

KARIN: I like you too, Petra, a lot, but you have to give me time. Please.

PETRA: I'll give you time, Karin. We have the time. We have so much time. We have time to get to know each other. We'll love each other—Marlene, bring us another bottle of champagne. (*Marlene exits.*) I've never fallen in love with a woman. I'm crazy, Karin, crazy! But it's marvelously wonderful to be crazy like this.

(*Blackout.*)

# ACT THREE

*It is early morning. Karin is lying in bed. Petra's just getting dressed. Marlene is cleaning up the breakfast things from beside the bed. Karin is reading a magazine.*

PETRA: Have you canceled the reservations?

KARIN: What?

PETRA: I asked if you've canceled the reservations?

KARIN: Why for God's sake? I'm sorry but I'm still lying in bed.

PETRA: Okay. I'll do it myself.

KARIN: I'll take care of it. Just let me wake up first.

PETRA: No, I can do it myself. Why shouldn't I? (*She goes to the telephone.*) Hello? I have reservations for two on the 25th to Madrid. For Kant and Thimm. Karin Thimm. You do? Okay. Unfortunately I have to cancel. No, not for the time being. Yes. Thank you.

KARIN: In fact you don't need to cancel flights. Either you're there or you're not. They'll find out soon enough.

PETRA: Common courtesy demands it, sweetheart. One day even you'll understand that.

KARIN: Thank you.

PETRA: You're welcome. Marlene!

(*Marlene enters.*)

PETRA: My shoes. Quick.

KARIN: I'm gradually coming to the conclusion she's nuts.

PETRA: She's not nuts. She's in love with me.

KARIN: Many happy returns. (*Marlene brings the shoes.*)

PETRA: Thank you. (*Marlene returns to work.*) Is it final then? You don't want to go back to school?

KARIN: What's "final" supposed to mean? I'm not studying any more.

PETRA: There's always something new to learn. It is an ongoing process.

KARIN: You with your pearls of wisdom.

PETRA: Not wisdom, experience. Look, I'll call up and make the excuses, then you can go back. I think it would be better for you just this once to see something through to the end. It always pays off, believe me.

KARIN: If you think so.

PETRA: Yes. I think so.

KARIN: Okay then.

PETRA: Fine.

KARIN: Fix me a gin and tonic, how about it?

PETRA: (*Fixing the gin and tonic.*) You drink like a fish. Be careful you don't get fat.

KARIN: Go fuck yourself.

PETRA: Don't forget your figure is your capital reserve. And it's all you've got.

KARIN: If you say so.

PETRA: I don't just say so, I know so. Prost.

KARIN: Prost.

PETRA: (*Sits on the bed beside Karin and embraces her.*) I love you.

KARIN: Me too.

PETRA: Bullshit. Me too. Me too. Say it for once! I love you.

KARIN: Yes, yeah.

PETRA: Come on.

KARIN: Okay I like you. I love you.

PETRA: You have the dreamiest skin in the world.

KARIN: Yeah?

PETRA: Yes. And the most beautiful hair, and shoulders, and . . . the loveliest eyes. I love you, I love you, I love you. I love you.

KARIN: Please leave me alone.

PETRA: But why?

KARIN: I haven't brushed my teeth yet.

PETRA: It makes no difference.

KARIN: It embarasses me. Come on. And I want to do some more reading. Please.

PETRA: Okay. I'll leave you in peace. If you are so disgusted.

KARIN: I'm not disgusted. But we can't be doing it twenty-four hours a day.

PETRA: Yes we can.

KARIN: Oh Petra.

PETRA: I could spend an eternity in your arms. I can't understand why you're so cruel to me. As if I'd done something to you. I'm only trying to help you.

KARIN: I'm not cruel.

PETRA: For you it's so easy. You just say, "I'm not cruel." But whenever I need you, you reject me. Karin?

KARIN: Yes?

PETRA: May I . . . I just want to be beside you a bit longer.

(*Karin doesn't respond. Petra sits on the edge of the bed. After a few seconds she begins to caress Karin.*)

PETRA: By the way, where were you last night? (*Karin doesn't respond.*) Karin?

KARIN: Hmmm?

PETRA: I asked you where you were last night?

KARIN: Dancing.

PETRA: 'Til six in the morning?

KARIN: So?

PETRA: Those places aren't open that late.

KARIN: No?

PETRA: No. Who were you . . . "dancing" with?

KARIN: What do you mean?

PETRA: I asked who you were dancing with, didn't I?

KARIN: With a man!

PETRA: What?

KARIN: Yes.

PETRA: What sort of man?

KARIN: A big black man with a big black cock.

PETRA: Well, well. (*She goes to the bar and makes another gin and tonic.*) Did you want another one too?

KARIN: Yes, make me another one.

PETRA: Gladly.

KARIN: But you don't have to if you don't want to.

PETRA: I *do* want to. And you could behave a little bit more friendly. Here you are.

KARIN: Thank you, dearest, thank you!!

PETRA: How was the man?

KARIN: In bed?

PETRA: Yeah, that too.

KARIN: Insatiable.

PETRA: Was he?

KARIN: Amazing. Imagine it. Big black hands on my fine white skin. And . . . those lips! Of course you know blacks all have those thick warm lips. (*Petra clutches at her chest.*) Fainting spell, dearest? (*Laughs uncontrollably.*)

PETRA: (*To Marlene.*) Don't gawk like that, you cow. Fetch the papers! Beat it!

KARIN: Now, now, why are you getting so hysterical? (*Marlene goes out.*) The best is yet to come.

PETRA: Don't be so mean.

KARIN: I'm not being mean. I'm telling the truth, Petra. At the very start we discussed the fact that we wanted to be honest with one another. But you can't it. You'd rather be lied to.

PETRA: Yes, lie to me. Please lie to me.

KARIN: So okay, it's not true. I was out walking alone the whole night and thinking about us.

PETRA: Were you? (*Hopefully.*) Is that true?

KARIN: Of course not. I did sleep with a man. But that's not so important, is it?

PETRA: (*Crying.*) No. No—of course not. But I don't understand, I really don't understand. Why . . . why . . .

KARIN: So quit crying, Petra, please. Look, I really like you, I really love you . . . but . . . (*She shrugs her shoulders. Petra cries with abandon.*) Look, it was clear all along. I was gonna be sleeping with men again. That's how I am, that's all. No problem for us. I just use them. That's all, really. A little fun. That's it. You were always sort of talking about freedom. You said we shouldn't be bound by obligations, neither one of us. Quit crying now, huh, I'm back with you.

PETRA: My heart is aching. As if it had been pierced through by a knife.

KARIN: Your heart don't need to hurt. That's not necessary.

PETRA: Doesn't need. *Doesn't.* I do need . . . you don't need . . . it *doesn't* need. My heart doesn't need to hurt.

KARIN: Oh, Petra. Of course I'm not as smart as you, or as educated. I know that, see.

PETRA: You're beautiful. I love you so . . . I love you so badly it hurts. Oh dear God. (*She goes to make herself a drink.*) Do you want another one?

KARIN: No. I have to watch my waistline.

(*They look at each other, spontaneously laugh for a second, then stop just as quickly. They look at each other a moment longer, then Petra pulls away.*)

PETRA: Are you going to see him again?

KARIN: Who? The same man?

PETRA: Yes. Or are there so many of them?

KARIN: Come off it.

PETRA: So?

KARIN: No. I won't be seeing him again. I don't even know his name. Besides. he said he's being transferred.

PETRA: Really a black man?

KARIN: Yes. Why?

PETRA: No reason.

KARIN: Hey, you know he was something. You'd have liked him. He wasn't exactly black, just kind of brown, and he had a real intelligent face. There are those blacks you know, and they have these Caucasian faces kinda, you know.

PETRA: Oh? I didn't know.

KARIN: Sure there are. That's what he was. He told me some neat things too, about America.

PETRA: Please Karin. (*She starts to cry again.*)

KARIN: Okay, I'll shut up. I thought we just worked it out though.

PETRA: You don't have to . . . revel in the whole business. ( *She makes herself another drink.*)

KARIN: Looks like you don't mind the sauce yourself.

PETRA: What else is left?

KARIN: Don't overdo it, goddammit. You're being downright hysterical.

PETRA: I'm not hysterical. I am in pain.

KARIN: Come off it. If you're in pain it'll do you good.

PETRA: Oh, yes, sure, it's so easy for you to say. If someone's in pain, then it's for their own good.

KARIN: It's true.

PETRA: I'd rather be happy, Karin, believe me. I'd much rather be happy. The whole thing is making me sick.

KARIN: What's making you sick?

PETRA: Drop it.

KARIN: No, tell me, what's making you sick?

PETRA: You. You make me sick. Because I never really know why you're here. Because I have money, or connections, or because . . . you love me.

KARIN: But of course . . . it's because I love you. Shit.

PETRA: Stop it. I can't bear this much longer.

KARIN: If you don't believe me . . .

PETRA: Believe you. What's that supposed to mean? Of course I *believe* that you love me. Obviously. But I don't know. I don't really know. That's what's making me sick. That.

(*Marlene comes in with the newspaper, gives it to Petra, and continues to draw. Petra opens the newspaper.*)

PETRA: Look at this: "Petra von Kant's latest collection is sure to make heads turn in the coming season." And a picture of you.

KARIN: No. Show me.

PETRA: There.

KARIN: Oh this is wild. Looks pretty good too, huh? Admit it.

PETRA: Yes, quite lovely.

KARIN: Quite lovely, quite lovely. It's *amazingly* wonderful. My first time in the papers. Wild. (*Embraces Petra, kisses her.*) I love you. Come on.

PETRA: Cut it out.

KARIN: I want to kiss you.

(*They kiss. The telephone rings and Marlene gets up. Petra pushes Karin away.*)

PETRA: I'll get it. Leave it. Von Kant. (*To Karin.*) For you! From Zurich.

KARIN: Zurich?

PETRA: Yes. Who do you know in Zurich anyway?

KARIN: I don't have a clue. Hello. This is Karin Thimm. Who? . . . Freddy!!!! You're in Zurich? How'd you get to Zurich? When? Three o'clock in Frankfurt? Hang on, I'll ask. When does the next plane leave for Frankfurt?

PETRA: (*Looks at her watch.*) Two thirty.

KARIN: The next plane from Cologne to Frankfurt leaves at two thirty. I'll try to get on it but if I can't, Freddy you call me again from Frankfurt. (*She turns to the side.*) I love you. Bye. (*She hangs up.*) That was my husband!!!! Freddy is in Zurich. Freddy's in Europe. Try to get me on a flight to Frankfurt, come on, please.

PETRA: (*Walks mechanically to the telephone. Karin gets up, dresses.*) Lufthansa? This is Petra von Kant. I would like to book the 2:25 flight to Frankfurt . . . completely booked?

KARIN: No!! Please, please . . .

PETRA: First class still has room? Good, then reserve a seat in the name of Thimm. Karin Thimm. An hour before take off, I know. Goodbye.

KARIN: Wild. Freddy here. Wild.

PETRA: (*Making another drink.*) You always used to say that you and your husband . . . you said there was nothing between you any more.

KARIN: That was such a long time ago, Petra, I . . .

PETRA: At least you could have . . . said that you . . . were still in touch.

KARIN: But he's still my husband. Naturally I wrote to him.

PETRA: You even said you both wanted a divorce.

KARIN: I said maybe some day we'd get a divorce. In six months you can have a change of heart.

PETRA: Do you know what you are?

KARIN: No, but you won't waste time telling me.

PETRA: You're a miserable stinking little whore. Stinking little whore.

KARIN: Is that what you think?

PETRA: Yes, that's what I think. A disgusting little creature. Just looking at you makes me want to puke.

KARIN: Then you're sure to be happy when I leave.

PETRA: Ha! But what took you so long? I wonder why you didn't get right down to it, and start pimping yourself sooner.

KARIN: Because with you, dearest, it didn't take as much exertion.

PETRA: Oh sure, now I understand. My God are you a creep. What kind of person willfully injures someone like that, when they see that other person has trusted them?

KARIN: I didn't deceive you Petra.

PETRA: Oh yes you did. You lied to me. You kept it all very hazy, what was going on between us. That's deceptive enough.

KARIN: I said I love you. That's not a lie, Petra. I love you. In my fashion You have to grant me that.

PETRA: I would have thought of the whole thing much differently from the very start if you had . . . how can you be such a creep, Karin? You saw what it meant to me. What was going on.

KARIN: That's not true. For a long time I had no idea "what was going on." At the very start you were behaving like it was just "fun." Admit it.

PETRA: (*Goes to Karin and embraces her.*) I can't help it that I love you. I can't help it. I need you Karin. I need you so much. (*She kneels down and clutches Karin's legs.*) I want to do everything for you. I want you to be the center of my being. I have nothing besides you. I . . . I . . . I'm so lonely, so alone without you, so lonely Karin.

KARIN: Lonely—with your . . . whore?

PETRA: Oh please, oh please forgive me. You have to understand what . . . I was . . . what I was going through. Don't be so brutal.

KARIN: Get up, I'm in a hurry.

PETRA: Why you filthy little pig. (*She spits in her face.*)

KARIN: You'll pay for that. I'll never let you forget it.

PETRA: (*Tries to embrace her again, but Karin rejects her.*) Karin I don't know what I'm doing any more. You have to understand.

KARIN: Give me some cash. I have to pay for the plane. And then there's Frankfurt: Freddy never has money.

PETRA: That's exactly what I'm good for. The payoff. God in heaven . . . Okay, how much? Just say.

KARIN: Five hundred.

PETRA: (*Fetches money from a drawer.*) There. A thousand. That should help the two of you get something together.

KARIN: I only need five hundred. Really.

PETRA: Don't worry about it. Take the thousand. What difference does it make now? (*She goes to the table and picks up her car key.*) Marlene, drive Karin to the airport. I'm too drunk.

(*Marlene and Karin go to the door. Marlene exits.*)

PETRA: Karin! Are you really leaving? Hm?

KARIN: Yes.

(*Petra sits down and cries. Karin approaches her and runs her fingers through her hair.*)

KARIN: I'll be back. (*Petra nods.*) Ciao.

(*Karin goes to the record player, puts on "In My Room," and leaves.*)

PETRA: (*Sobbing with abandon; to the end of the song.*) I'm so stupid. So stupid.

(*Blackout.*)

# ACT FOUR

*Petra is alone on stage. She is already drunk, trips over a carpet, etc. The Platters' "The Great Pretender" is heard on the record player. She dances to the music, and sings along. Makes herself another drink. The telephone rings. Petra runs and answers it.*

PETRA: (*In a hopeful tone of voice.*) Hello? No this is not Frau von Kant. (*She throws down the receiver, sits down in an armchair and drinks. The telephone rings again and she quickly picks it up.*) Yes? No, no, no, no. (*She hangs up.*) I hate you I hate you I hate you . . . I hate you. If I could only die. Just be gone. This suffering. I can't stand it. I . . . I just . . . I just can't stand it any more. God the father in heaven what a bitch. What a stinking little bitch. I'll get even some day. I'll wipe your face in it, really wipe your face in it. You're going to lick my boots, you little whore. Crawl at my feet. Christ am I fucked up. Dear God, what did I do to deserve this? What? (*The telephone rings.*) Karin?! (*She hangs up.*) I love you so much. Don't be mean to me, Karin! Oh shit. Shit. I need you badly. At least call me, please call me at the very least. I just want to hear the sound of your voice. (*Crying, she crosses to the bar and makes a drink.*) It won't cost you anything to call me. A simple phone call. It can't cost much. But it won't even occur to that pig. It's all calculated, calculated. She wants to keep me waiting because . . . oh it's all so sordid. You disgust me. Just a dirty little shit. And I'm crazy in love with you. Crazy in love! If you only knew how much it hurts. I hope this happens to you some day, that you're reduced to this. You'll see things a little differently then. You are so stupid. A total idiot. We could have had it so nice together. It would have been so fine. You'll realize it, some day. But then it'll be too late. Much too late. Believe me, I'll get my revenge.

(*The doorbell rings. Petra runs to get it.*)

GABI: Mama! A very happy birthday to you.
PETRA: Oh Gabi!

(*Petra, Gabi and Marlene enter.*)

GABI: Hasn't grandma arrived yet?
PETRA: No.
GABI: I have such an enormous amount to tell you.
PETRA: Yes my dear little girl. Of course. Marlene, make us a cup of coffee.
GABI: My God you wouldn't believe the flight we had. The plane was wobbling all over the place. I nearly got sick to my stomach. Oh mama, it's been so long since I've seen you. Dear dear mama. Four months. Isn't Karin here?
PETRA: No!
GABI: No? But she'll be back. Won't she?
PETRA: No, I don't think she will.
GABI: No matter. I'm not so fond of her anyway.
PETRA: No?
GABI: Well, you know she is actually . . . rather common, don't you think?
PETRA: No. That she is not.
GABI: Oh, what's the difference. Mama, I'm so unhappy.
PETRA: Unhappy?
GABI: No, actually I am incredibly happy. I don't know, mama. It's all so confusing.
PETRA: What do you mean, my little girl?
GABI: Mama—I'm in love!
PETRA: You are . . . (*Starts to laugh uncontrollably.*) No, that's altogether too comical. You're in love.
GABI: I find your response to this appalling, mama. Decidedly bourgeois. Really.
PETRA: I'm sorry, truly. But for me you've always been a little child. I will have to get used to the idea that you've grown up.
GABI: Please. Oh mama.
PETRA: Tell me, Gabi. Tell me all about your boyfriend.
GABI: That's just it, mama. He isn't even my boyfriend yet. He doesn't even have the slightest idea that I'm in love with him. You wouldn't believe the way nothing gets through to him. For three weeks I've been trying to flirt with him, and he cuts me every time. It's as though I didn't even exist. Mama, it's awful, so awful.
PETRA: Believe me, it'll be alright.
GABI: Oh mama, he's so good looking. You can't imagine how good looking he is.

PETRA: Want to bet? He's tall, slim, has blond hair and looks a tiny bit like Mick Jagger.
GABI: How did you know?
PETRA: Aha—*that* I will not reveal.
GABI: Oh mama, you're so smart. I have the smartest mother in the world.

(*The telephone rings. Petra leaps to her feet, runs over and picks it up.*)

PETRA: Yes? No!!! (*She hangs up, sits down in the armchair next to the telephone and sobs.*)
GABI: Mama, mama. Who was it? (*Petra cries.*) Oh, mama, mama. Say something. What's the matter? (*She cries too.*) Don't cry, mama. What happened?
PETRA: Nothing, Gabi, nothing. Stop crying. Nothing has happened, really. (*Sobs again, gets up, goes to the bar and makes a drink. Marlene enters with the coffee. Mother and daughter hide their tears, but Marlene nevertheless notices that something is wrong and stays where she is.*) You can see to the pastry now, and the whipped cream. (*Marlene stays—Petra yells.*) Get out of here and see to the pastry and the whipped cream. Or can't you hear properly? Out!! (*Marlene exits.*)
GABI: Why do you treat her so badly, mama?
PETRA: Because she doesn't deserve any better, and she doesn't want it any differently anyway. It makes her happy, can't you tell?
GABI: No.
PETRA: Don't be absurd. You shouldn't worry yourself over the help.
GABI: I don't want to quarrel with you on your birthday, mother, but you know that I definitely do not share your views in this matter.
PETRA: Good for you. Children should be free to develop their very own thoughts. That is the current wisdom, isn't it?

(*The doorbell rings. Petra tries to answer it, but Gabi cuts her off.*)

GABI: Let me get it. (*Petra is tense and expectant. Gabi returns.*) May I present: the Baroness Sidonie von Grasenabb.
SIDONIE: Petra! Darling!
PETRA: Sidonie!
SIDONIE: Best wishes on your birthday. I mean it, from the heart, Petra. (*Hands her a gift.*) Open it later. How are you doing in school, Gabi?
GABI: "C" average I guess, Aunt Sidonie.
SIDONIE: Well a "C" average, yes, sufficient, quite sufficient.
PETRA: Marlene! Another cup, hurry!
GABI: I think mama mistreats Marlene, don't you?
PETRA: Gabi!

SIDONIE: Gabi, I agree with your mother that you are too young to be passing judgment on her behavior.
GABI: Great. Then I'll shut up.
SIDONIE: Dearest. How *are* you?
PETRA: How should I be? Just fine.

(*Marlene brings Sidonie's tea.*)

SIDONIE: Thank you. Well let's hear it. I read about your success in Milan. Congratulations.
PETRA: You know the whole pile of shit bores me to tears.

(*Gabi laughs.*)

SIDONIE: Don't laugh.
PETRA: Let her laugh.
SIDONIE: As you wish. Your mother says you are to laugh.
PETRA: You know I'm fed up with this job. Design, show, show, design—and always afraid it won't catch on. For what? The same thing again and again.
SIDONIE: Quite simple. Survival, Petra. You have to work to make money, and you need money to live.
PETRA: Precisely. In the old days I enjoyed the work. But I got exhausted. Had enough. Finito. (*Screams.*) The pastry!! She's doing it on purpose to annoy me.
SIDONIE: That's not true, Petra.
GABI: I wish she would.
SIDONIE: Gabi! Don't say such things.

(*Marlene enters with the pastry, puts it on the table, leaves. A somewhat awkward pause ensues.*)

SIDONIE: Have you heard from Karin?
PETRA: From Karin? No, and you?
SIDONIE: Yes, I know she has a job with Pucci.
PETRA: With Pucci, huh?
SIDONIE: Yes indeed. She's talented, that girl. She'll get on just fine. I'm sure of it.
PETRA: Talented? She's not talented, Sidonie. She knows how to sell herself.
SIDONIE: I'm not sure you are being fair. Perhaps we're being a little bit subjective in our judgment, hmmm? By the way, she's in Cologne today.
PETRA: She is? . . . Well *darling* aren't we well informed!
SIDONIE: I want to be honest with you, Petra. Karin called me this morning. Otherwise I wouldn't have had a clue she was here.

PETRA: Of course I told her it was your birthday, dearest. And she did say she'd try to drop in on you, but couldn't be certain, because she was tremendously busy.

PETRA: Tremendously busy? Sure, I know.

(*She goes to the bar. Sidonie gets up and follows.*)

SIDONIE: Don't drink so much. You have to take care of yourself, Petra. In this world it's too easy to let oneself go under.

(*The doorbell rings. Stunned, Sidonie and Petra stare at the door. Gabi runs out, and returns with Petra's mother.*)

VALERIE: You must excuse me Petra. It took me forever to get a taxi. All the best on your birthday. Were you expecting someone else?

PETRA: No!

VALERIE: Well then, let's sit down and have a nice little chat. Sidonie, my child, you get younger every day.

SIDONIE: Cheers, Auntie Valerie. That comes from being happy. Quite simple.

VALERIE: The traffic in this city will be the death of me yet. Honestly. How's school going, Gabriele?

GABI: Okay.

VALERIE: Do I detect strife in the air?

GABI: They won't let me talk, grandma.

SIDONIE: Gabi you know that's not true.

GABI: You refused to let me express my opinions. True or false?

SIDONIE: No one refused to let you do anything. That's a lie, pure and simple.

GABI: You did too. You wouldn't let me say what I wanted.

SIDONIE: What a wretched little child.

VALERIE: Calm down children. Let's all be nice to one another.

(*Petra smashes her glass on the wall. Marlene comes running in. She picks up the shattered glass.*)

VALERIE: Petra!

PETRA: Each and every one of you makes me want to puke.

SIDONIE: (*Stands up.*) That's quite enough, Petra.

VALERIE: Sit down, please. What's troubling you then, my child.

PETRA: You're all such phonies. Smelly little phony little shits. You haven't got a clue.

GABI: Mama!

PETRA: And you . . . loathesome child. I hate you. I hate all of you.

GABI: Mama. Oh, mama.

PETRA: Don't touch me. Marlene, make me a gin and tonic. If you only knew how vile you were. Prost! Parasites, a swarm of parasites.

VALERIE: What's wrong with her?

SIDONIE: Oh the poor thing.

PETRA: I am not a poor thing. I'm just seeing you with fresh eyes. And what I see makes me want to vomit. (*She smashes the glass.*)

VALERIE: Stop it, now! You are wrecking the whole apartment.

PETRA: So what. Did you work for it? You haven't lifted a finger in your whole life. First you lived off father, then me. You know what you are for me? A whore, Mother, a miserable, filthy, rotten whore.

VALERIE: Oh Petra, Petra!

(*Petra upsets the coffee table.*)

GABI: Mama.

PETRA: I'll destroy whatever I damn well please. I earned it. Do you understand that or don't you?

VALERIE: I'm confused, completely confused. What did we do to you?

SIDONIE: It's because of the girl.

VALERIE: What girl? What are you talking about?

SIDONIE: Karin.

VALERIE: Because of Karin? What about Karin?

SIDONIE: Everyone knows Petra is crazy about Karin.

PETRA: Crazy? Crazy's the wrong word, Sidonie. I'm in love with her. I love her like I've never loved anything in my life.

VALERIE: You love her? You love a girl? Oh, Petra, Petra.

PETRA: That girl's little finger is worth more than the rest of you put together. Karin, Karin.

GABI: Mama, please. Mama.

PETRA: Get away from me you cretin. Gin and tonic, Marlene. Ten gin and tonics.

VALERIE: My daughter in love with a girl! A girl! My daughter! God this is awful.

(*The telephone rings and Petra runs to it.*)

PETRA: Karin?! (*Hangs up.*) Oh no, no. I can't stand it. I can't stand it. I want to destroy everything, everything.

SIDONIE: Calm down, Petra.

PETRA: What do you care anyway? To you it's amusing. Good gossip material for a year. Shut your face. I feel so rotten. OhGodohGodohGod-ohGodohGodohGod.

SIDONIE: I'm leaving. I don't have to put up with this. Honestly.

PETRA: So go then. Beat it. (*She pushes and shoves her.*) You think I care about you? I never want to see you again for the rest of my life. Never. You understand that? Never again.

SIDONIE: I'm going to make you pay for this, Petra. Absolutely. You're not going to get away with it.

PETRA: I'm not paying for anything any more. I atone for enough as it is. Who's next? Who else wants to leave? The door's open. Beat it, all of you, beat it. I don't have anything more to give you. I'm out of it. Gin, gin Marlene. Or do you want to get lost too? What do you have to cry about? Huh? What? You're all happy. All of you. Happy. (*She falls to the floor.*)

VALERIE: My child. My poor, poor child.

PETRA: I want to die, mama. I want do die, really. There's nothing worth living for anymore. Death . . . so peaceful, and calm, and beautiful. So peaceful, mama. Everything so peaceful.

GABI: Mama. Mama. I love you so very much.

PETRA: It just takes a few pills, mama. You wash them down with water and you sleep. It's so nice to sleep, mama. I haven't been able to sleep for so long. Oh I want to sleep . . . to have a long, long, long sleep.

(*Blackout.*)

# ACT FIVE

*Petra is sitting in an armchair; Marlene is drawing at the easel. Valerie enters.*

VALERIE: Gabi's asleep now.

PETRA: I'll pull myself together, mother.

VALERIE: The panic, when it comes, always makes us vulnerable.

*(She goes to the bar and makes two drinks. Gives one to Petra.)*

PETRA: Thank you.

VALERIE: You came into this world approximately thirty give years ago. Gabi has had a shock.

PETRA: Spare me, mother.

VALERIE: That is not a reproach, Petra. But you have to know. I visited your father's grave. Someone put flowers on it. That's the second time it's happened.

PETRA: I was afraid you would hate me because of Karin.

VALERIE: I know. Perhaps I would have, who knows. Thirty-five years ago it was raining. Big drops splattering the windowpane.

PETRA: I'm terribly frightened, mother. So alone.

VALERIE: I visit father's grave a lot these days. Much more often than I used to. I'm going to church again too.

PETRA: I haven't even been enjoying my work for a half year or so. And constantly . . . the feeling that my head is about to explode.

VALERIE: It takes courage to have faith, Petra. We all need God. To be comforted in him. All of us. Without God . . . we are so lonely.

PETRA: No mother. There is no comfort in that. What we need is to love someone—to love them without making demands.

VALERIE: It's the same thing, Petra. Believe me.

PETRA: It wasn't love I felt for her. I just wanted to possess her. Only now, that it's all over, am I beginning to experience love. This has taught me a lot, mother, and caused me a great deal of suffering. I had to learn, but should it have to hurt so much?

VALERIE: Be kind to Gabi. Children are so sensitive.

PETRA: I know.

VALERIE: She cried so hard before she went to sleep. You must let her get closer to you.

PETRA: Stop torturing me mother. What good does it do you?

VALERIE: I must speak my mind. (*The telephone rings. Valerie picks it up.*) Petra von Kant residence. Who? Just a moment please. (*She covers the phone.*) Karin.

PETRA: (*Gets up slowly, takes the phone.*) Karin? Thank you. Fine. Tomorrow? Yes. Chang's? Okay. 'Til tomorrow then. Bye bye. (*She hangs up, remains standing.*) You can go now mother. I've calmed down. I'm at peace again. I'll call you.

(*Valerie picks up her things and exits without a word. After a moment Petra puts on a record. She remains standing while listening to the music. After the music is over:*)

PETRA: I need to atone, Marlene. For all I've done to you. In the days to come we'll work together—really together—and you can enjoy yourself, just as you deserve. (*Marlene gets up, crosses to Petra, goes down on her knees and attempts to kiss her hand.*) No, not like that. Let's sit down together. (*They sit.*) Tell me about your life.

(*Blackout.*)

END

# Bremen Freedom

CHARACTERS:

Geesche Gottfried, as it turns out, a businesswoman
Miltenberger, her first husband
Timm, her father
Mother
Gottfried, her second husband
Zimmermann, a friend
Rumpf, a friend
Johann, her brother
Bohm, a cousin
Luisa Mauer, a friend
Father Markus, a priest

*The action takes place in Bremen, around 1820. For meticulous directors, Bremen currency at the time was as follows:*

$$1 \ Taler \ = \ 36 \ Groats$$
$$1 \ Groat \ = \ 24 \ Schwares$$
$$360 \ Groats = \ 1 \ Pound \ of \ fine \ silver$$

*Geesche, Miltenberger. Children crying.*

MILTENBERGER: Paper . . . Coffee . . . Brandy . . . Shut the windows . . . Quiet!
. . . Bread and gravy . . . Salt . . . On the 31st of October, 1814 we shall lay
to rest our beloved mother, Clara Mathilde Beez, née Steinbacher, taken
from us by the good Lord . . . Quiet! . . . Brandy . . . This constant yowling
will be the death of me . . . More coffee . . . So the beheading is to be Friday
—November 3, 1814, in the market square . . . Brandy . . . When I say brandy woman, I mean the bottle and not a few measly drops . . . Here's to you
. . . Cigar . . . Light . . . Too hot in here . . . Oh to have one evening of
peace in this house . . . Quiet! . . . Shut the windows . . . *Another* ghost spot-
ted in Bremen . . . We don't *need* the fire that intense . . . Strange things oc-
curing in this city . . . Prepare my nightcap, this headache is . . . Quiet! . . .
My medicine.
GEESCHE: I want to sleep with you.

*(He looks at her. A long ominous pause. Then he sets the newspaper down, slowly
rises, approaches Geesche. For a moment one has the feeling he wants to embrace her,
but then he starts hitting her, quite brutally, until she lies sobbing on the floor. He
stands over her. A knock at the door. Miltenberger opens. Gottfried, Zimmermann
and Rumpf enter. They are very drunk. Gottfried notices Geesche and goes to her.)*

ZIMMERMANN: We were just passing by, brother.
RUMPF: This place could be a distillery, there's so much liquor around.
MILTENBERGER: The better to serve my friends. Make yourselves comfortable.

ZIMMERMANN: No sooner said than done. Rather cold out there.
GOTTFRIED: Your wife . . . ? She's lying on the floor crying.
MILTENBERGER: One of her fainting spells. Geesche! Brandy!

(*Geesche slowly gets up, exchanges a glance with Gottfried, then exits to fetch the brandy.*)

RUMPF: Sit down, Michael Cristoph. Gather ye rosebuds while . . .
ZIMMERMANN: Hear about Redheaded Rhea? They've shut her place down.
MILTENBERGER: Shut it down?
RUMPF: Shut it down. Three of the girls are infected.
MILTENBERGER: They're . . . infected.
RUMPF: VD, Johann.
MILTENBERGER: VD . . . no, that's not . . . which girls?
ZIMMERMANN: Carmen.
MILTENBERGER: No.
ZIMMERMANN: Gesina.
MILTENBERGER: No.
ZIMMERMANN: Marieluise Annegrat.
MILTENBERGER: No again.
RUMPF: Three no's! None of us! We're off the hook!
ZIMMERMANN: I'll bet it won't be long before one of our solid Bremen citizens is the proud father of a syphilitic brat.

(*They laugh uncontrollably.*)

MILTENBERGER: Geesche!

(*Gesche quickly enters. She has obviously fixed herself up. She serves the brandy.*)

MILTENBERGER: Get on your knees and offer a prayer of thanks for the good health and good fortune of your children's father.

(*Geesche kneels down in front of the crucifix and prays. The others laugh.*)

ZIMMERMANN: (*Through his laughter.*) A man is strangling the mother of his children, with bare hands. Her eyes bug out of her head, naturally. He asks her, ice cold tone of voice, hey what do you think you are staring at?

(*Laughter. They guzzle water glasses full of brandy.*)

MILTENBERGER: A man's going at it with a woman, gets carried away and bites her tit. Afterward he says, don't blame the kid on me. Which kid? You're pregnant, you're filled up with milk. Milk? You've got it all wrong. That was a boil, but thanks anyway for popping it! (*All except Gottfried laugh.*) You have to see just how much my wife loves me. Geesche! Come here. Say I love you.

GEESCHE: I love you.

MILTENBERGER: Say, I want you.

GEESCHE: I want . . . (*She runs away. He catches her. Embraces and kisses her.*)

MILTENBERGER: Say it!

GEESCHE: (*Softly.*) I want you.

(*They all laugh. Geesche cries.*)

MILTENBERGER: (*Returns to his seat.*) My wife. She knows who's boss. Get some brandy. (*Geesche exits.*) She knows the meaning of humility. And in bed, Jesus Christ she goes at it like a wild mare in heat. Just right for someone who's got what I do.

(*Geesche returns with the bottle. As she takes it to the table Miltenberger grabs her and kisses her. She half-heartedly fends him off, but he persists. They all continue drinking.*)

RUMPF: There's an execution on Friday. I almost get hard the split-second before the axe . . .

ZIMMERMANN: What's going through the condemned man's mind—the last few seconds, what does he feel, what . . . it's crazy.

GOTTFRIED: I'm going home. It's been a long day.

(*He gets up, followed by the others.*)

RUMPF: So. We're off. Until tomorrow, Johann Gerhard. Work. Make a living. Ah well.

ZIMMERMANN: 'Til next time.

(*They make their farewells. The three leave.*)

MILTENBERGER: Geesche. Come here.

(*She remains still. He staggers towards her. She tries to evade him, but he catches her, and proceeds to paw her. She is clearly disgusted.*)

MILTENBERGER: Don't be absurd, woman. You have to learn who's master in this house. Who has a right to his little pleasures.

(*He wrestles her into the bedroom. Knocks her down again. Kisses her.*)

(*Scene change—through lighting or other methods. Miltenberger enters, utters a scream, agonizes during the following.*)

MILTENBERGER: Help me. I'm on fire. Geesche! Geesche!

(*Geesche enters, casts a doleful glance at her husband who is doubled over in pain.*)

MILTENBERGER: Don't just stand there. Help me! Get a doctor!
GEESCHE: (*Slowly shakes her head, kneels down in front of the crucifix and sings.*)

World, farewell! of thee I'm tired,
Now t'ward heav'n my way I take;
There is peace the long desired,
Lof-ty calm that nought can break:
World, with thee is war and strife,
Thou with cheat-ing hopes art rife,
But in heav'n is no al-loy,
On-ly peace and love and joy.

(*While Geesche is singing, Miltenberger lets out horrifying animal-like screams and a few garbled words. He dies.*)

MILTENBERGER: Geesche . . . the doctor . . . I love you . . . Geesche . . . you can . . . Geesche . . . my belly . . . I'm . . . I . . . dying.

(*Geesche turns around, makes the sign of the cross over her dead husband, kneels down and prays in silence. Then she drags Miltenberger offstage. Geesche's father, Timm, enters, and restlessly paces the stage. He is dressed in mourning clothes.*)

TIMM: My dearest husband . . . I would like to announce . . . a cross to bear . . . death . . . it is the dear Lord's way of . . . bitter tears . . . the pain, the awful suffering . . . gall bladder infection . . . on the first of this . . . Geesche!

(*Geesche enters, also dressed in black.*)

TIMM: You took long enough.
GEESCHE: I'm sorry, father.
TIMM: Sit.

(*Geesche sits at the table, picks up pen and paper.*)

TIMM: On the first day of this month . . . the good Lord claimed my . . . my dearly beloved and never to be forgotten husband.

*(Geesche's mother enters. Geesche runs to her and they embrace, the pair of them sobbing.)*

TIMM: Sit down, Geesche. Duty first.

*(Geesche sits. Her mother squats on a stool, stares ahead, and quietly sobs.)*

TIMM: Where were we?

GEESCHE: My dearly beloved and never to be forgotten husband . . .

TIMM: My dearly beloved and never to be forgotten husband, comma, Johann Gerhard Miltenberger, semicolon, barely . . . how old?

GEESCHE: Barely thirty-three years of age, comma, and in the . . . *(he counts)* eighth year of our harmonious and gratifying wedded life, comma, blessed by the good Lord with four children, comma, two of whom preceded him into eternal life, comma, his earthly sojourn came to an end, comma, due to a severe gallbladder infection, that's fine, period. Convinced, open parenthesis, even before receiving public condolences, close parenthesis, that all who knew him will join with me . . . in tears and in the hurt . . . with which I, comma, together with his closest friends and relatives, comma, will follow his coffin to the grave, yes, what now? New paragraph? New paragraph. I would merely like to add . . . what about the business?

GEESCHE: I'll ask Michael Cristoph Gottfried, father.

TIMM: A good man to see you through, Geesche. You can look for something permanent later. Good. Well then, how far have we got?

GEESCHE: I would merely like to add . . .

TIMM: Yes. I would merely like to add the following brief note, colon . . . Be it herewith understood that the business of the dear departed will continue in the hands of a highly qualified party, comma, and that I will make every effort comma, as ever, to fulfill the trust of those who honor me with their custom. Period. Geesche Maria Miltenberger, comma, née Timm.

GEESCHE: Mother, oh mother!

*(She jumps up and runs to her mother. They embrace. Her father proofs the dictation. A knock at the door. Father answers it. Gottfried, Zimmermann, Rumpf, Frau Mauer and possibly a few others arrive to offer their condolences.)*

MAUER: Geesche! My poor dear friend.

GEESCHE: Luisa.

RUMPF: *(Breaking up their embrace.)* Most honored and respected lady I wish to offer you all the sympathy and support you deserve.

GEESCHE: Thank you, Rumpf, thank you.

ZIMMERMANN: I share Herr Rumpf's sentiments exactly. My heartfelt sympathies. *(She quietly squeezes his hand.)*

GOTTFRIED: I too would . . . (*He squeezes her hand, remains silent, as they stare at each other.*)

GEESCHE: May I ask you a question, Gottfried? Would it be possible for you, at least temporarily . . . to look after my husband's business. Please.

GOTTFRIED: I'll have to . . . yes, dear lady, yes.

(*They are transfixed, staring into one another's eyes. All but Geesche and Gottfried make their exits. Once they have gone:*)

GEESCHE: I love you. (*They embrace, kiss.*) I . . . I've been . . . I've been waiting so long . . . Michael.

(*Lights, etc. A change. Tableau reminiscent of the opening one with Geesche and Miltenberger.*)

GOTTFRIED: That Arthur is just too slow. He is not productive enough.

GEESCHE: But he *is* capable.

GOTTFRIED: Capable, sure Geesche, but slow . . . Coffee . . . If a worker is slow at his job, Geesche, skill or no skill, management must . . . quiet . . . must turn its mind to certain alternatives.

GEESCHE: Tell me, what are the alternatives your mind has turned to?

GOTTFRIED: I think it's inevitable. The firm needs to grow. Expand or go under, that's what I say. I think we should hire another saddler. Arthur will do the quality work for the older, established customers. The second worker will be for the new trade. Quick jobs for people on the move.

GEESCHE: Another saddler? We'll have to pay him. He'll need food and lodging.

GOTTFRIED: Think it over. If it's possible to make a living from one saddler, think how much better off we'd be with two?

GEESCHE: Makes sense. Yet . . .

GOTTFRIED: No "yets" about it, Geesche, and not a single "but." I have already considered the difficulties. We must expand our base of regular customers. That much is clear. *How* to accomplish that will have to be worked out. There's no problem calculating the surplus orders we'll need to float the additional worker . . . Paper! . . . Now the orders come in at roughly one thousand Talers per month, which in itself is too much for one man to handle. Rent 200 Talers, wages 250 Talers, materials 50 Talers, which leaves us 500 Talers per month. Each hour of Arthur's labor nets him—let's see, 15 hours a day times 26 days that's 390. He gets 65 Groschen an hour. Double that for us makes 130 Groschen. Understand?

GEESCHE: Not quite.

GOTTFRIED: One more time. For each hour Arthur works he gets 65 Groschen, but you get 130. With two employees we pay out 130 Groschen per hour. However, we earn, at the rate of 260 per hour.

GEESCHE: It's so simple. Splendid.
GOTTFRIED: You husband was stupid. To tie himself to the workbench when he had capital in reserve! What he spared in wages he paid in good health . . . Coffee.

(Geesche fetches him coffee, serves it.)

GOTTFRIED: Paper . . . Quiet!

(Geesche brings the newspaper.)

GEESCHE: I love you!

(Gottfried doesn't respond. She walks behind him and runs her fingers through his hair.)

GOTTFRIED: Please, Geesche. It's broad daylight. Night time is when people make love.

(A knock is heard. Geesche opens the door. It is her mother. They embrace, kiss one another. Gottfried puts the paper down, makes his apologies, exits.)

GEESCHE: Happy birthday, Mother.
MOTHER: Geesche! Geesche.
GEESCHE: Mother?
MOTHER: The torment your father is putting me through!
GEESCHE: Father?
MOTHER: That I'm putting myself through, since I even find it difficult to commune with God. I spoke with him, and have accepted the burden of guilt.
GEESCHE: What guilt?
MOTHER: The guilt of allowing a child of mine to live in sin.
GEESCHE: Mother! (Geesche tries to embrace her mother, but is rejected.)
MOTHER: No, Geesche, don't touch me. You're living with a man without benefit of the Sacrament. You are not a good Christian mother if you cannot spare your children this shame.
GEESCHE: Listen to me, mother. Please. I am being true to my feelings, that's all. I love him. There's nothing evil about it.
MOTHER: That a woman could let . . . let a man . . .
GEESCHE: Make love to her, mother. Say it.
MOTHER: Women have to stifle these ideas the moment they arise. My child, when you were just this big didn't I guide you on the correct path to womanliness? Explain to you over and over again the meaning of propriety? What you are, and what a man is, and what he thinks . . . There is simply no

comparison.

GEESCHE: (*Shouts.*) That is not true! Mother, for your entire life you have believed a lie.

MOTHER: Geesche! You are toying with mortal sin!

GEESCHE: No, mother, no. There's nothing sinful in what I have to say. I am in love with a man. I've always loved him.

MOTHER: Geesche!

GEESCHE: (*Growing louder and more intense.*) I love him, mother and I don't care what the world says. I want him to mount me.

(*Her mother, continually yelling "Geesche stop it," runs toward the door, but Geesche blocks her path.*)

GEESCHE: No you don't! This time you stay put, and listen to me. I want that man, in my bed. I don't sleep with a sacrament. I sleep with arms, and shoulders. I sleep with legs, mother with . . .

MOTHER: Geesche!

GEESCHE: No matter, what you are saying doesn't affect me. I have no will of my own that I am aware of, nor would I know how to assert it. How can I help it that you've wasted your life doing someone else's duty.

(*Long pause.*)

MOTHER: (*Subdued tone.*) Your sin is inscribed in your face, Geesche. The courts would brand you a heretic for talking that way.

GEESCHE: Mother, sit by me, and I'll lay my head on your lap, and be your little girl again. Please. Mother. Come.

(*They sit together and Geesche rests her head on her mother's lap.*)

GEESCHE: You see, mother, you want your Geesche to be happy. You really do.

MOTHER: Oh but Geesche, you know that God is the source of all happiness. Only by obeying his commandments can you be happy. Earthly happiness bars the way to eternal bliss.

GEESCHE: I am living in the here and now, mama. Name me the person who can guarantee there *is* an afterlife?

MOTHER: You are possessed, Geesche. By an evil spirit. Words to the Godless, wasted breath!

(*Mother cries. Geesche slowly rises, walks to the crucifix, makes the sign of the cross, continues on to the stove.*)

GEESCHE: Coffee, mother. Have a cup. (*Geesche gives her mother some coffee. One*

*cannot really make out whether she has put something in it or not.*)
MOTHER: How have I sinned, oh Lord, to deserve this? A child of mine! God-
less. My child. (*She slobbers through these lines while drinking coffee.*) I'm feeling
dizzy. Better go home. Cry there. I'll talk with God and ask him not to be
too harsh with the child who has so vilified him. (*The old woman leaves,
weeping, unsteady on her feet.*)
GEESCHE: (*Geesche pours out the rest of the coffee. Kneels before the crucifix, sings:*)
World, farewell! of thee I'm tired,
Now t'ward heav'n my way I take;
There is peace the long desired,
Lofty calm that nought can break.

(*Father runs in. He is upset.*)

TIMM: Geesche. Mother is dead.

(*Geesche slowly turns around, faints. Father affectionately takes her up in his arms
and carries her off stage. Lights dim, etc. Gottfried enters reading a newspaper.*)

GOTTFRIED: Quiet! I am really losing my patience. Quiet!

(*Geesche enters. She is dressed in black. Meek demeanor. Gottfried looks at her. She
averts her eyes, sits, cries.*)

GOTTFRIED: Your father's good at this. Listen. On the second day of the
month, on her birthday, my dearly beloved spouse, Geesche Margarethe
Timm, née Schaefer, fell victim to an intestinal inflammation and departed
this busy life. Quiet!
GEESCHE: Michael!
GOTTFRIED: What? It's true, damn it!
GEESCHE: Michael!
GOTTFRIED: Despite manifold domestic vicissitudes, we have spent these last 32
years together in the perfect contentment of a happy marriage, one which
has been blessed with two children. The pain I feel at her loss is unrelenting,
as she is irreplaceable, in this life. Only trust in providence and the prospect
of a better future life can give any value to my remaining days, which I shall
devote to my children and grandchildren. Bremen. Johann Timm. Clean.
That, Geesche, will drive up business.
GEESCHE: (*Slowly turns and looks at him.*) Can you imagine what mother's life
was like, Michael? No? Father writes "in the perfect contentment of a happy
marriage." No, not for mother. She wasn't satisfied a single day in her life.
Happiness for mother—that meant solace in the bosom of the Lord, not
father's bosom. She was his drudge, and his housepet. Her lot was obe-

dience. The only freedom she knew was in her conversations with God.
And they call that a happy marriage! She never had her way, she had to
answer his every whim—*his* whim, and he could smack her or hump her as
he pleased. Very cozy for father. *That's* what he calls his "great loss."
Mother didn't have a life, Michael. Death was a blessing.

GOTTFRIED: Coffee and something to eat . . . you think too much for a woman.
Too much of a strain, Geesche. You'll get wrinkles, grey hair.

(*She turns, gives him a long look. He is preoccupied with the newspaper.*)

GOTTFRIED: Geesche?!
GEESCHE: Yes?
GOTTFRIED: I . . . I find it hard to say this. I know . . . well, to be blunt . . . I'm
going to be looking for my own apartment again.

(*Geesche's hand makes a quick subtle move to her heart.*)

GOTTFRIED: I am fed up with the children, the noise, Geesche. And I need a
woman with whom I can have my own children. I can't stand it, Geesche,
seeing another man's children in the house. There's a lot I can't stand. I
need a young girl, someone fresh, and who doesn't have all these ideas in
her head, you know—someone caring and hard-working. I will continue to
manage the business as long as you need me, although . . . (*He looks at her.*)
Yes, well.

GEESCHE: (*Somewhere between hysteria and a state of collapse, with tremendous intensity.*) You told me you loved me. Often.

GOTTFRIED: Yes, Geesche, but . . .

GEESCHE: No! You say you love me. Then you're fed up and it's too much for
you. How is that?

GOTTFRIED: Yes, Geesche. I love you. I love your passion, and I respect your
mind, and yet . . .

GEESCHE: What in this world could be more important than love between two
people? Once you find someone you love . . . do you really think that happens every day? It is so rare, Michael, it is enough to make you despair.

GOTTFRIED: Love does *not* make the world go round. Something you females
easily get confused about.

GEESCHE: No, Michael. Life is bearable only if one has a center, a home. And a
woman's home is her man.

GOTTFRIED: You're in a state of despair, Geesche. You'll come to your senses.

GEESCHE: Scum! My God, that is what you are: Scum.

GOTTFRIED: Believe me, Geesche, the darkest hour is that before the dawn.

GEESCHE: (*Straightforward.*) You already have someone, don't you?

GOTTFRIED: No, Geesche. But I'll keep my eyes open, get to know a few young ladies, weigh their pros and cons. I need a challenge to keep me interested.

(*Geesche throws herself round his neck, cries. He strokes her affectionately.*)

GOTTFRIED: Calm yourself. You are bound to find happiness again. You have money, and a business on top of that. Believe me, that's a drawing card . . . The business is ticking over, yields an ample profit. It'll get better too, Geesche. Mr. Right will come along, don't you worry.

GEESCHE: I love you. I love your hands, and want them to touch my body. I want to feel you inside me. I need your passion. The very *thought* that you're leaving hurts, hurts deeply. Have you ever felt the pain of despair, the gripping in your stomach that goes with it? Never? You ought to. It would give you a new perspective. (*Pause.*) Don't leave me.

GOTTFRIED: Can't you see Geesche, I yearn for another kind of life. I am a man, and men have desires that women don't understand. Can't you appreciate how I ache to have my own child?

GEESCHE: We can have one *together*! We're both fertile. What's stopping us from having our own child, Michael?

GOTTFRIED: God almighty, Geesche, I am not about to see *my* children and your husband's growing up together. I want to provide them with their own home, give them a proud, upstanding life.

GEESCHE: The world has gone made. Two people. In love. And it's utterly hopeless.

GOTTFRIED: You'll get over it soon enough. I'm going in to town to have a drink. Back in a while.

(*Gottfried turns in the door, shakes his head, then leaves. The children are crying, off. Geesche breaks into tears, controls herself, goes out to the children. After a few seconds they cry even louder. Geesche returns, kneels in front of the crucifix and starts to sing. During the second strophe the children suddenly grow quiet. Deadly quiet.*)

GEESCHE:

World farewell!—Of thee I'm tired,
Now t'ward heav'n my way I take;
There is peace the long desired,
Lof-ty calm that nought can break:

World, with thee is war and strife,
Thou with cheat-ing hopes art rife,
But in heav'n is no al-loy,
On-ly peace and love and joy.

When I reach that home of gladness
I shall feel no more this load,

Feel no sickness, want, or sadness,
Resting in the arms of God.

In the world woes follow fast,
And a bitter death comes last,
But in heaven shall nought destroy
Endless peace and love and joy.

(*Lights fade, etc.*)

(*Intermission.*)

(*Geesche, Timm and Gottfried returning from the burial.*)

TIMM: This house deserves every ounce of misery it gets.

GEESCHE: Father!

TIMM: I know what I'm saying, Geesche. Break His commandments, and suffer God's wrath.

GEESCHE: That's enough. You are an old man and no longer understand the world. Go home.

TIMM: Yes, that's how children speak to their parents nowadays. No respect for age. Wisdom and experience? Hah! They've become nuisances. No, Geesche, this won't bring you peace of mind.

GEESCHE: Peace means death, father, and I want to live. I can't see myself longing for peace.

TIMM: In my whole life I have never known a woman to say such a thing. What have I done to deserve a child who could—so brazenly and blasphemously talk back to her father?

GEESCHE: I'm not talking back, father, and I'm not brazen. I'm speaking my mind.

TIMM: Women who speak their minds are in ignorance of the law. The law which forbids it. You there, Gottfried. Nothing to say to me? (*Pause.*) Silence talks! Set yourself up in business here, didn't you? Saw the opening and jumped in. Made a good living for yourself. But the decent thing to do—to marry the woman who set you up, who gave you the opportunities in the first place . . . that would be asking too much. You turned my daughter into a whore, and she's too dumb to see it. But you're a man, you have intelligence. In your heart you know what you are: a criminal.

GEESCHE: Father!

TIMM: Don't interrupt when men are talking. Nothing to say? Gottfried! And I was under the distinct impression you were a gentleman.

GEESCHE: Please father, stop it. He'll make up his mind when he can. He's not prepared to be tied down yet.

TIMM: Some *man*, who lets his woman do the talking!

GEESCHE: Father, just let us straighten out our own lives. We'll obey the law, I promise.
TIMM: I've said enough. There's no point. When two people so blatantly disregard all morality, they can expect *nothing* but endless misery. And as for me, I only hope the tears you shed will cleanse your eyes, and make you fit to see God's truth.
GEESCHE: Oh, father.
TIMM: Put your life in order, or do without a father. Don't forget my words. My child, from this moment you are completely alone in the world. That man is using you, he has nothing to give.

(*Timm exits, weary and shaking his head.*)

GEESCHE: Father! Can you forgive him? Michael? The suffering of these last two years has affected his mind. He's lost all perspective. First a son-in-law, then his wife, and now two grandchildren—of course he's obstinate. Forgive him. Please.
GOTTFRIED: Yes, Geesche. I've already forgiven him.

(*Pause.*)

GEESCHE: Michael?
GOTTFRIED: Yes?
GEESCHE: Essentially . . . what father's saying . . . is right.
GOTTFRIED: How do you mean?
GEESCHE: I mean . . . basically if the two of us . . . you and I . . .
GOTTFRIED: Get married?

(*Geesche nods silently.*)

GOTTFRIED: No, Geesche. Not now, and I *do* want to be honest: perhaps never. I don't really know what I feel about you, or where I stand anymore. I know I love you, and yet . . .
GEESCHE: And yet?
GOTTFRIED: I can see myself living without you. I've always thought that to be in love, totally in love with someone, would make it impossible to think of living without them.
GEEESCHE: I can't. But me . . . I don't count.
GOTTFRIED: Not true. You do count. After all, I'm here and I have respect for your love and for all the suffering. Besides, I'd have left if that wasn't the case. I thought, "she has just buried both her children, you can't leave her in the lurch to boot." I was thinking of you, not me. I love you, truly, in my fashion.

*(While he speaks, Geesche begins to sob quietly. Gottfried goes to her, puts his arms around her, caresses her. Lights dim to change scene, or something similar.)*

*(Lights up.)*

*(Geesche and Gottfried remain in an embrace, as at the end of the last scene.)*

GEESCHE: We're going to have a baby.

*(Gottfried tosses her on to the couch.)*

GOTTFRIED: Say that again.
GEESCHE: We're going to have a baby, Michael, our baby.
GOTTFRIED: But you always said you were using a pessary.
GEESCHE: Yes but it happened when you came back from Hanover a day early. I couldn't have known.
GOTTFRIED: That is deceit, Geesche. Deceit, you understand. To let a man think he can sleep with you carefree, and . . . what an idiot I am, to fall for that kind of thing.
GEESCHE: The way you're taking this. I might have known . . .
GOTTFRIED: *(Mocking her.)* "I might have know, I might have known." God, are you stupid. The tiniest mental effort and you'd have seen I wanted out.
GEESCHE: Oh, Michael.
GOTTFRIED: Look at yourself. *(He takes hold of her and drags her to the mirror.)* Have a good look. Is that something a man would want to live with? With that dishrag for a puss? That expression? *(He throws her to the floor.)* My God, you are repulsive. Had I been able to guess that one human being could be so disgusted by another human being, then I'd have known that you were to be the woman in my life.

*(Geesche gradually picks herself up, looks in the mirror, fixes her hair.)*

GEESCHE: Well then, fine. Now it's happened. What do you have in mind next?
GOTTFRIED: Take a look at yourself. Look how hardened you've become. Any self-respecting female would be stretched out on the floor right now, totally destroyed, and weeping hot tears.
GEESCHE: What good would that do me, Michael? Humm? What good would that do me?
GOTTFRIED: It would get you some sympathy. And sympathy can pass for love.
GEESCHE: I don't need sympathy, Michael. And besides, the tears I've wept . . . Mary Mother of God. You sat there, reading, and never noticed what was going on in the person who loved you. You say I disgust you. That's alright. And despite that, Michael, I'm carrying a child in my womb, your child.

You ought to figure out what to do because before long it'll be showing.
GOTTFRIED: I want no part of it. (*He runs off, she chases.*)
GEESCHE: Michael!

(*Lights out. Geesche helps Gottfried on to the stage. Gottfried is shaking and groaning. She is very tender toward him. She arranges the couch for him, covers him.*)

GEESCHE: Father Markus should be here any minute, Michael. Would you like another drink? I love you so much. Believe me, you'll be well again. It won't last forever.

(*Knock at the door. Geesche goes to the door, opens it. Father Markus enters.*)

MARKUS: Got here as soon as I could. (*Sits by Gottfried.*) Greetings, Herr Gottfried. Are you in pain? (*Gottfried nods.*) Thank your lucky star you have a woman like this to tend to you. I can tell you some stories. Be that as it may. You never know whether you're getting what's coming to you, or . . . Are we ready?

(*Gottfried nods. The priest looks at Geesche.*)

˙ GEESCHE: Yes, father. Yes.
MARKUS: We are here assembled to join together this man and this woman in the sacrament of holy matrimony. Do you, Johann Michael Gottfried, take this woman, Margarete Geesche . . .?
GEESCHE: Miltenberger, née Timm.
MARKUS: Yes, of course . . . take this woman, Margarete Geesche Miltenberger, née Timm, to be your lawful wedded wife, to have and to hold, in sickness and in health, 'til death do you part? Say "I do."
GOTTFRIED: (*Struggling.*) I do.
MARKUS: And you, Margarete Geesche Miltenberger, do you take this man, Johann Michael Gottfried, to be your lawful wedded husband, to have and to hold, in sickness and in health, 'til death do you part? Say "I do."
GEESCHE: I do.
MARKUS: I hereby pronounce you man and wife, 'til death do you part.

(*Gottfried dies.*)

GEESCHE: Father! (*She drops to her knees and inspects Gottfried. Looks up.*) He's dead.
MARKUS: The marriage is legitimate. No question.
GEESCHE: He's dead, Father. Dead. (*She rolls around on the floor. The priest makes the sign of the cross.*) Dead, dead, dead. He's dead. (*She controls herself.*) Sing

with me. (*They kneel in front of the crucifix.*)
GEESCHE AND MARKUS: (*The song, duet.*)
World, farewell! of thee I'm tired,
Now t'ward heav'n my way I take;
There is peace the long desired,
Lof-ty calm that nought can break:

World, with thee is war and strife,
Thou with cheat-ing hopes art rife,
But in heav'n is no al-loy,
On-ly peace and love and joy.

GEESCHE: I want to confess, Father.
FATHER MARKUS: Yes, my daughter.
GEESCHE: I gave him poison, Father, to make him sick and to force him to give the child I'm carrying, his child, a good name. Father, I didn't want to see him die. It was an accident, Father. God in heaven knows what I was thinking! I have been pregnant four months and the father refuses to acknowledge that it's his. That drives a woman insane, Father. She can't control her thoughts. You lose perspective. What's good is evil and the evil good. You cry nights on end into your pillow and you pray to God for help . . . which never comes. Can you imagine how alone you are when no one listens? Father, how lonely and utterly abandoned? The God doesn't exist who knows what that's like and who would still turn a vengeful eye on the wretched woman. Loneliness, dear Father, is the worst thing in the world.

(*Timm enters. The priest stands.*)

MARKUS: You are too late. I have joined your daughter and Michael Christoph Gottfried in holy wedlock. He died shortly thereafter.
GEESCHE: Oh, father. (*She runs to her father, and embraces him.*)
TIMM: My child. My poor, poor child.
MARKUS: My fee for services rendered is exactly twenty Gulden.

(*Geesche breaks into a fit of laughter. The priest makes the sign of the cross.*)

TIMM: Come to my place. I'll pay.

(*The two exit. Geesche controls herself again. She kisses Gottfried on the forehead, and with much effort drags him offstage. Once there, we hear a cry which doesn't seem human: "Geesche suffers a miscarriage."*)

(*Lights dim, etc. Geesche enters with Timm and Bohm.*)

TIMM: Geesche, prepare some coffee and do what you can to make Herr Bohm

feel comfortable. He's my nephew from Hanover. A saddler.
GEESCHE: A saddler?
TIMM: A saddler, Geesche. I gather you take my meaning. Frankly, I was think-
ing he could take over the business. Besides, he likes you.
GEESCHE: Him?
TIMM: Frankly, he asked for your hand, Geesche, and he's a gentleman. I ac-
cepted, with heartfelt pleasure. Your life will be smooth sailing from now on.
Say goodbye to the chaos your life has become—no more sorrow, embarrass-
ment, dishonor.
GEESCHE: Oh, father, Your little girl has outgrown the old morality. She can
find a bed-partner on her own.
TIMM: Geesche!
GEESCHE: No, father. Don't shout.
TIMM: I'll shout at my daughter whenever I like. You think you can run the
business? A woman? Do you really believe that?
GEESCHE: Yes father, I'm quite sure of it. I know more about this business
than anyone. And I'm not just going to hand the whole thing over.
TIMM: I lent your first husband 1200 Talers so he could open the saddle shop.
1200 Talers! That's *my* money supporting *your* business.
GEESCHE: I have enough. I'll buy you out.
TIMM: No, Geesche. I didn't come here to discuss, I came to inform. The dec-
ision has been made.
GEESCHE: I hear what you are saying, father. Still, I won't obey. I am a human
being like every other human being and I can make my own decisions. Right
now I'm not interested in this man. Nor any other man. When the itch bet-
ween my legs needs something like a man to satisfy it, I'll go looking.
TIMM: Hold your tongue Geesche. The shame that kind of talk makes me feel
. . .
GEESCHE: Shame! Hah! Honesty makes you feel shame.
TIMM: I'll teach you. In the law-courts. You'll learn all about fathers' rights
over their daughters.
GEESCHE: Here, drink some of this coffee. It'll relax you.

(*Timm and Bohm drink coffee.*)

GEESCHE: If a woman's heart's not in it she's no good to you, cousin.
BOHM: No. (*He glances at Timm, who gives him a hard look.*) Yes she is.
GEESCHE: Yes or no?
BOHM: No.
GEESCHE: There you are, father. Cousin is a man of intelligence. He sees ex-
actly what he'd be getting into. Do you think he'd enjoy the good life with a
woman who didn't love him? She'd burn the roast, water his brandy. She'd
make bitter coffee, and in bed she'd lie there like a two by four. Lead that

sort of life and what does it get you?

BOHM: I don't want this woman, uncle Timm. Not any more. She's too smart for a man like me. I want to run things in my house. In this place I'd just be a servant.

TIMM: Come on Bohm. Let's go. You'll pay for causing me this disgrace Geesche. You'll pay.

GEESCHE: Not any more, father. I won't be doing the paying ever again.

(*Once they have gone, Geesche makes the sign of the cross in front of the crucifix. Song. During the song Zimmermann appears. Geesche doesn't notice him, and he creeps up behind her and puts his arms around her. She is startled, but they lie together on the floor and kiss.*)

GEESCHE: Zimmermann! You could scare a body to death.

ZIMMERMANN: Females don't die that easily.

GEESCHE: You're crazy. Oh God that's good, oh . . .

ZIMMERMANN: I . . . love you.

GEESCHE: Wait. Let's use our heads. Someone might drop in . . . then what . . . ?

ZIMMERMANN: If you say so . . . Look, Geesche, it's horrible.

GEESCHE: Horrible? What?

ZIMMERMANN: Sooner or later I have to tell you.

GEESCHE: Well say it. Spill out your heart. There's always hope. Always.

ZIMMERMANN: It's my brother you see, he . . . no that's not the way it goes. When my father died he left his sons 20,000 Talers apiece to set themselves up in life. I had the wife's business so I didn't need it, the cash I mean. My brother, fourteen years my junior . . . no, that's not right either. The money I was just talking about, that's the money I lent you. So far so good. Now my brother he wants to . . . he's made an offer for a property which he could secure for the 20,000. Geesche, I know it might be hard for you just now, but it's father's last will, and I do want to respect it. You're a clever woman. You should be able to understand.

GEESCHE: You need your money, the 20,000?

ZIMMERMANN: That's how it is, my brother and all, Geesche . . .

GEESCHE: I understand what you said, perfectly, just . . . it won't be possible.

ZIMMERMANN: Not possible, Geesche?

GEESCHE: Not possible, Zimmermann. It's like this. I have already invested the money, in a new workbench, and tools, lots of new items. That can increase the profits of course, though . . . that hasn't been the case so far.

ZIMMERMANN: I guess you haven't quite understood. I am not making a request, Geesche. I am laying down a demand.

GEESCHE: A demand. Yes, of course. But if nothing's there to take . . .

ZIMMERMANN: I want my money back. Sell, Geesche. However you do it, I don't care. I want my money and that's final.

GEESCHE: But you love me.

ZIMMERMANN: In money matters, best forget love, Geesche.

GEESCHE: No Zimmermann. Answer the question: do you love me?

ZIMMERMANN: Whether I love you or not has nothing whatsoever to do with my money.

GEESCHE: Drink your coffee and we'll discuss the matter in a civilized manner.

ZIMMERMANN: (*Sits, drinks.*) Alright then. What do you propose?

GEESCHE: Zimmermann, it's very simple. The business nets . . . 800 Talers per month, half of which—yes, half—I need for myself, to keep up the house, to buy clothes and so on. The other half, the remaining 400, that I can pay back to you, as regular installments. That's my offer.

ZIMMERMANN: Ridiculous. It would take, at 4800 a year . . . nearly 5 years . . . absolutely ridiculous.

GEESCHE: Remember, Zimmermann, you *gave* me the money. There was no talk of paying it back.

ZIMMERMANN: That was in the heat of passion, Geesche, when a man talks too much and sometimes even *does* stupid things. I will expect to be informed by Friday when you plan to repay the money—three months, that's as long as I'll wait, otherwise it's mortgage the saddle shop. You'll see what I'm really like, Geesche. (*He gets up.*)

GEESCHE: I'll see you out . . . Good luck. (*On the way she hums the melody.*)

(*Geesche enters with her brother, Johann Timm.*)

GEESCHE: The misery in this house, it never lets up, Johann. Hardly ever.

JOHANN: How . . .?

GEESCHE: You mean, how could it have happened? I can't explain it. All I can do is give the details. The first to die was my husband, Johann Gerhard Miltenberger—gallstones. Shortly afterwards, mother died of an intestinal inflammation. Then the two children, Johana and Adelheit, of a lung infection and typhus; followed by my second husband, Michael Christoph Gottfried, after a brief illness, and last of all father, for no particular reason, just the years taking their toll, I guess. Oh, Johann, you've been away so long, it must be a great shock to you that we've had to endure so much.

JOHANN: Yes, Geesche. I thought I'd come home and find the family just as I left it. When you are away from home, you wonder how the people back home are doing. I've seen so much death in the war I'm not shocked by it any more. But the loss—parents, in-laws, nieces—that's hard. I'm just happy you're still here. If I came back and no one was alive and no one remembered Johann Timm—how could I bear that?

GEESCHE: Oh, Johann!

JOHANN: Geesche! (*They embrace.*) My dear little sister. How you must have suffered. How many tears these eyes must have shed. I had planned only a short stay in Bremen, then I was going to find myself a new war. But now—I can't leave my sister alone, leave all this hard work to a woman. I'll take over the business, Geesche, don't worry.

GEESCHE: (*Cries out in shock.*) No!

JOHANN: No! Geesche!

GEESCHE: Johann, you know I had to struggle to master this business. I had to study, hard. And now that fate has left me so alone in this world the business has become . . . my life, Johann. I want to make it clear that you'll get your rightful share. I don't want anything that doesn't belong to me, but I do stand firm on this point: *no one* takes my work from me, thank you.

JOHANN: Little sister, little sister, you're just a woman. Women can learn plenty of things, but they can never enjoy work. You'll soon get used to keeping house again. You'll be humming a tune while you tend the stove, not a worry in your head. Work would only toughen you. It'd destroy your softer, feminine qualities. And of course you'll be wanting another man to take to your bosom.

GEESCHE: The man *I* want to take to *my* heart—I'll tell you what he'd have to be like. He'd have to accept the fact that women can think, that they have the power of reason. Maybe the man hasn't been born yet who can do that, in which case I'll do without.

JOHANN: Geesche, I . . .

GEESCHE: Let me finish, Johann. I was put on this earth to use my brain, and to express my thoughts without interruption. Take it calmly, Johann. Nice and calm. Listen to me. I will not simply hand over the business. Never. I'll live my life the way I want. To *live* a life, that's what all human beings should strive for. And women are human beings too, even if the men and women who recognize that are few and far between.

JOHANN: Geesche, you are giving me a migraine. What you are saying here . . . I can't accept it.

GEESCHE: Learn it, Johann, or be on your way.

JOHANN: (*At the top of his lungs.*) I go when I want, Geesche. And I do what I want. A woman! That's the last thing I'd let dictate to me. Especially my sister. I will take over the business, Geesche, as sure as I am sitting here. That's my final word, I'll say no more. (*Pause.*)

GEESCHE: I'll give you a nice cup of tea to warm you up, brother. (*She gets up and pours him a cup of tea.*)

JOHANN: See. That's what I admire in a woman. Care and devotion—hard work. But all this *mental* effort, where's that going to get you?

(*Geesche gives him tea, adds the sugar, stirs. He drinks it in one draught.*)

JOHANN: I'm going to bed, Geesche. Wake me early, please. I want to get on with learning the business.

(*He leaves. Geesche makes the sign of the cross in front of the crucifix. Begins to sing the song, but the lights dim quickly.*)

(*Lights up, etc. Frau Luisa Mauer enters.*)

GEESCHE: Luisa, dearest Luisa.

LUISA: Geesche! You grow younger and more beautiful each time I see you. How do you manage it?

GEESCHE: Freedom, dear. Freedom, plain and simple.

LUISA: Is that so? How splendid. But are you sure of that?

GEESCHE: Quite sure, dearest Luisa. Sit down.

LUISA: Someone like you, who has had so much suffering and misfortune, yet managed to remain so unaffected, she must be . . .

GEESCHE: Yes?

LUISA: She must be in league with the devil, wouldn't you say?

GEESCHE: The devil?

LUISA: How else can a woman . . . such as me make sense of a creature who undergoes so much, yet remains in the pink of it? A small cup of coffee Geesche, please. That you are never short of men who willingly enter this hell, it's terrible.

GEESCHE: Terrible?

LUISA: Terribly exciting of course. I regularly make bets with my Friedrich about who'll be the next one to drop dead in this house. Incredible suspense, dear, and yet it never fails to surprise us, really.

GEESCHE: (*With coffee.*) Here you are.

LUISA: Thank you, dearest, thank you. As a matter of fact, I put my money on your father, and who was it? Your Gottfried. It's so easy to fool oneself.

GEESCHE: Indeed. It's so easy to fool oneself.

LUISA: Isn't it ever?! And your breasts, my dear, fuller and firmer as time goes on. How do you do it?

GEESCHE: Padding, my dear.

LUISA: Padding?

GEESCHE: Yes, padding. I know what men like, what excites them right off. And . . . I can't sleep unless I have a man with me.

LUISA: Oh, retch, Geesche, retch.

GEESCHE: Retch, Luisa? Why that?

LUISA: People don't really say what they're thinking, just right out like that. But then, *excuse* me—with you anything goes, right?! And these perpetual affairs—all out in the open, no discretion—a woman has it pretty good like that, huh? Don't you agree with me? To be honest I wouldn't want to be like you. I've been with my husband fifteen years. He has a mind of his own, and he gets the job done. He can ask me anything, and I'll do it. I will.

GEESCHE: Have you never once felt the desire to know more about the world than you do now?

LUISA: Never.

GEESCHE: And have you never thought how lovely it would be to be released from your "background?"

LUISA: Geesche . . . the way you talk, and the ideas you have.

GEESCHE: Answer me please.

LUISA: No, of course not. I'm feeling ill, Geesche. It's bad.

GEESCHE: That's from the poison in the coffee you just drank.

LUISA: Poison?

GEESCHE: In the coffee.

LUISA: Oh, oh is that ever the limit! A joke. And appropriate coming from you.

GEESCHE: It's no joke, Luisa. I've poisoned you. Really.

LUISA: You've . . . No, no, you . . . you can't do that.

GEESCHE: Yes dearest, quite definitely.

LUISA: And . . . and . . . why? Just tell me why?

GEESCHE: I wanted to save you from the kind of life you're having to lead.

LUISA: (*Screams.*) Help!

(*She runs to the door, but drops dead before she reaches it. At that moment Rumpf arrives.*)

GEESCHE: She's . . . she's dead.

RUMPF: Yes. Well.

GEESCHE: She just collapsed, and died. How terrible.

(*She tries to embrace him.*)

RUMPF: I went to the police and had them analyze the white cubes you put in my coffee. You wanted to kill me, Geesche, why?

GEESCHE: (*Shrugs her shoulders.*) Now I'm going to die.

(*She kneels down and sings all the strophes of the song.*)

(*Slow dim.*)

END

# Katzelmacher

## [For Marieluise Fleisser]

In Bavaria *Katzelmacher* is a derogatory term for an immigrant worker, the implication being that his sexual behavior is that of a tom cat.

CHARACTERS:

Helga
Gunda
Elisabeth
Marie
Ingrid
Paul
Jorgos
Bruno
Erich
Franz

*This play ought really to have been about older people. But it was to be done at the "antiteater." They're all young at the moment.*

R.W.F.

ERICH: Thirsty.

MARIE: I'll go for a beer if you want. But you give me the money.

FRANZ: Get me one too.

PAUL: Me too. She's not bad, gotta admit. Get in yet?

HELGA: Pauly!

ERICH: Get in? Pa-arty time! No comparison.

HELGA: You don't need to talk like that. You guys never quit. No respect, none of you.

PAUL: Ever get laid on respect? I doubt it.

MARIE: Here you go. Beer. The cultured folks say "thank you!"

PAUL: More to culture than "thank you's," believe me.

MARIE: If you don't know nothing, you ought to shut up.

ERICH: You said it. They cut my pay. Because things ain't what they were, they said. So what do you do? Shut your trap.

HELGA: So what if a girl you went to school with owns a factory.

ERICH: Plattner? Her? She has *one* employee. And what do they make? Wonder-bags!

HELGA: Wonderbags beat shovelling someone else's shit.

ERICH: I don't shovel shit. I drive a tractor, and I could get a factory, just like that one.

PAUL: For Christ's sake, when's the train gonna get here . . .

MARIE: Probably on time, if you wanna know.

FRANZ: If they had a dance here once a week thing's be a lot better.

ERICH: We already talked it over with the boss. Thinks he'd go down the tubes on it. Him and his ugly puss.

HELGA: Think yours is any prettier.
ERICH: Than his? You bet. People'd come from all over once it got started.
FRANZ: A group'd cost too much.
PAUL: What about a juke box?
ERICH: Wouldn't draw. There's jukeboxes all over the place.
FRANZ: They even got one in the Crown.
HELGA: But that space ain't big enough. Don't talk to me about dancing in
    there.

(Jorgos enters.)

ERICH: Looka' the way he's lookin'.
MARIE: What's his breed do you think?
PAUL: Sportin' fur on his lip too!
MARIE: Well?
ERICH: Got me!
HELGA: He's coming over.
PAUL: Can I help you, then?
FRANZ: Lose somethin'? Huh?
MARIE: What's your breed pal?
ERICH: Can't you answer when you're spoken to?
PAUL: Huh!
HELGA: Lookin' for someone? Someone in particular?
PAUL: What an eyeful! A real goof.
FRANZ: Maybe he doesn't want to talk to us. Maybe we're not good enough for
    him.
ERICH: You're supposed to open your mouth and S-A-Y some-thing!
JORGOS: Then Katalavo!
HELGA: A foreigner.
ERICH: See?
PAUL: S'what I figured.
FRANZ: Probably an Italian.
ERICH: Ithakan.
HELGA: So what are you? Italian?
JORGOS: No Italy.
PAUL: Na, that's an Italian through and through. He's Italian.
MARIE: Then what's he doin' here?
FRANZ: Yeah, that's what I'd like to know.
ERICH: Just shows up. And won't talk.
HELGA: Has to be headin' somewhere.
PAUL: He's Italian.
HELGA: Still gotta be goin' somewhere.
ERICH: Right.

HELGA: Where you goin'?

PAUL: Goin' to? Where?

HELGA: Address no? . . . Elisabeth Plattner and Co.

PAUL: To Elisabeth's. I knew it!

HELGA: I'll show you the way. Come. Come on!

PAUL: Yeah, on accounta she went to Italy last year. And now this thing's turned up.

MARIE: Gonna be consequences.

HELGA: Come over here to Elisabeth's. I always said she was man-crazy. Just look at him.

PAUL: Because we're not good enough I guess.

FRANZ: You anyway.

PAUL: Uh-uh. You.

FRANZ: He's nuts.

PAUL: An Italian from Italy.

HELGA: I don't believe she'd have the balls. But my mother always said it, don't fool with that Elisabeth. Always.

PAUL: An Italian from Italy.

MARIE: The train.

HELGA: I'm happier stayin' here. We need to talk it over with the people from around here.

PAUL: Come on.

***

ELISABETH: Now first we need to get the paperwork out of the way. Social security and the other deductions. You can sleep here, and that'll get deducted too. I had you brought in because the crowd in this town isn't worth a damn except maybe Bruno, him you'll meet, because they're all fatheads. Ok. The work's easy to learn but you gotta be fast, because otherwise production is down. Besides the salary they have the nerve to ask for! Where do they get off? There are so many bums around here, refugees left over, and all sorts of others. Meals you take here too, also deducted. Sperr worked here for a week, they buzzed non-stop over that, and then with Bruno, same thing, but we're used to it now. So when they talk, you just get used to it, ok. I was looking for someone ambitious, because if you're lazy you won't earn a thing. Now you know it all.

***

ERICH: Who we talkin' about?

PAUL: The Italian.

ERICH: Right.

GUNDA: So? What about him?

PAUL: He's Italian. That's all. (*Bruno enters.*) Ok. What's the story?

BRUNO: Ain't no Italian.

PAUL: No?.

BRUNO: A Greek. From Greece.

ERICH: No kiddin'? But Elisabeth never went to Greece.

BRUNO: But that don't have nothin' to do with him, because he's "foreign labor."

ERICH: What that?

BRUNO: Like I said, "foreign labor."

ERICH: What's that supposed to mean? Don't we have enough workers?

PAUL: A Greek from Greece.

ERICH: No way. That ain't fair no how.

GUNDA: Right.

ERICH: We work too. Plenty.

PAUL: He cut in on you yet, with Elisabeth?

GUNDA: Where's he sleep?

BRUNO: My room.

ERICH: Your room. How come?

BRUNO: There was a bunk, that's how come.

PAUL: Did he talk to you yet?

BRUNO: He can't talk. But when he goes to bed he strips. All the way.

PAUL: No!

BRUNO: Right.

GUNDA: With you there?

BRUNO: He doesn't know any better.

ERICH: What's he look like?

BRUNO: Better than us.

ERICH: How better?

BRUNO: Better built.

ERICH: Where?

BRUNO: In the cock.

(*Pause.*)

PAUL: They got a TV down at the Crown now. I'm heading over.

GUNDA: I'm going. See you.

ERICH: See you. What's on?

PAUL: Top ten, that kind of thing.

*** 

GUNDA: You're from Greece?

JORGOS: Greece.

GUNDA: You like it here? I asked if you're pleased with it here.

JORGOS: No understand.

GUNDA: Germany good?

JORGOS: Much good.

GUNDA: No much love?

JORGOS: No understand love.
GUNDA: From the heart.
JORGOS: No.
GUNDA: No? No girls?
JORGOS: What girls? Fucky-fuck?
GUNDA: Yes.
JORGOS: No not.
GUNDA: Why? Because of me?
JORGOS: Yes not.

*** 

INGRID: I heard it from Erich, and he got it from Bruno I think. Last night she took everything off, spread out on the bed and yelled for the Greek.
HELGA: Then what?
INGRID: Then the Greek came over, and three hours later he left again, and he looked completely wiped out.
GUNDA: I'm on my way home, and the Greek's coming towards me the other way. I say "hello," because I'm polite. He lays hold of me, shoves me in the grass and keeps saying "fucky-fuck." 'Til I nearly dropped dead. Then I ran away.
FRANZ: We're in for it now, with his foreign habits.

*** 

ELISABETH: You get nothing for nothing. You have to work faster, if you want to get paid.
JORGOS: Work not good?
ELISABETH: Work good, but not fast.
JORGOS: Understand. Work faster.
ELISABETH: Right. Hard work gets good pay.

*** 

PAUL: And then he raped her. In the field.
ERICH: Gunda? He ain't got no taste.
MARIE: I don't think he'd do it. He always has his eyes staring straight ahead.
ERICH: Got the hots for him?
MARIE: I'd never get the hots for him, but the way someone looks with his eyes, there's a reason for it.
PAUL: I'm tellin' you he threw her down on the ground and raped her, and the others will be next. I'm telling you.

*** 

HELGA: Walkin' arm in arm with him right in town. Both of them laughin'.
GUNDA: It's going too far with them. I shoulda gone to the police, that would have been the right thing to do.
HELGA: If he touches me he's had it.
GUNDA: Right thing'd be to kill him.
HELGA: Yeah but Elisabeth'd stick up for him. And she has pull with the big-

wigs.

GUNDA: If I slept with a chief of police like she did I'd have pull too.

HELGA: Old as he was. And how old was she then? Seventeen.

GUNDA: No shame. We should wipe that kind out, just wipe them out. The time'll come.

***

MARIE: I feel the kind of love they sing about in the songs.

JORGOS: Love much good.

MARIE: But they always keep talking. About you and Elisabeth.

JORGOS: Elisabeth no.

MARIE: I want to be the only one you go with, because a girl needs it that way.

JORGOS: Eyes like stars.

MARIE: Eyes like stars. That's pretty.

JORGOS: Holding nice.

MARIE: Was it nice with the other ones too?

JORGOS: No understand.

MARIE: In Greece girls pretty?

JORGOS: Yes pretty. In Greece much pretty. Come Greece together. Much sun and sea.

MARIE: Take me with? Honest?

JORGOS: Really. Much love.

MARIE: I love you too. I feel it, it hurts me so much, definitely.

***

ELISABETH: Have you been spreading it around that I do nothing but chase after him?

BRUNO: Ain't said a word. I wouldn't say anythin' about you because I couldn't anyway.

ELISABETH: I see it already when I walk through the neighborhood, the shit-eating friendly way they say hello to me.

BRUNO: I didn't say nothin'. Nothin'.

ELISABETH: Funny, they've never been spiteful like that before.

BRUNO: I could never talk about you like that, and you know it. Because my love comes first.

ELISABETH: He's getting better on the job. He's learning slowly—

BRUNO: But I'm still better.

ELISABETH: With your hands.

***

PAUL: Now he's knockin' off your Marie.

ERICH: She can suck my dick with her yappin' about marriage all the time. Why would I want to marry her? She's nuts.

PAUL: What about Ingrid?

ERICH: Nose in the air. She don't think marriage is her thing because it'll get in the way of her future plans. No feelings neither. With her you don't talk, you fuck. Good too.

PAUL: Helga's gonna have a baby.

ERICH: Really?

PAUL: Like I said. Three months gone.

ERICH: Weren't careful.

PAUL: She said she couldn't have a kid, a doctor in Munich told her, and now I'm sunk. My father's gonna have a heart attack when he finds out. I coulda killed her when she told me, she's always so snotty, Helga.

***

FRANZ: Over where he comes from they got communists.

INGRID: In Greece?

FRANZ: Read it in the papers. Lots of communists.

INGRID: Lots?

FRANZ: Right. Greece is full of commies.

GUNDA: Ingrid heard it from Franz, then she told me.

HELGA: You never know what's up, do you?

GUNDA: You get mixed up in things and you don't know how it's gonna turn out. Because commies are always dangerous.

***

ERICH: He's a communist and shouldn't be allowed.

PAUL: Because that just goes to show how it all fits in.

ERICH: And shouldn't be allowed.

PAUL: Barges his way in, and there he is, one of them.

ERICH: Shouldn't allow it, and it's bein' dealt with, don't worry.

***

FRANZ: What part of Greece you come from anyway? What city?

JORGOS: Pirea.

FRANZ: What's that like?

JORGOS: Much sun and sea and many come from other country.

FRANZ: And not much work.

JORGOS: Work yes, money no.

FRANZ: How much you making from Plattner-head?

JORGOS: No understand.

FRANZ: How much money? Here?

JORGOS: Two hundred twenty mark. Eat and sleep.

FRANZ: Oh yeah? She gave me three hundred twenty, plus food. Not for this guy!

JORGOS: Send all home. Wife, children.

FRANZ: You married?

JORGOS: Wife, children.

FRANZ: How many kids you got anyway?

JORGOS: Two.

***

HELGA: You having it off with a married man who has kids too?

MARIE: If you say so.

GUNDA: I'd be ashamed of myself and all you know about what kind he is and all.

MARIE: What kind is he?

GUNDA: A criminal and everyone knows it.

MARIE: Not with me he ain't.

HELGA: Because you're evil.

MARIE: I can do what I want with my lovelife.

GUNDA: Because he's a pig and grabs it where he can.

MARIE: Because he didn't want you.

GUNDA: Didn't want me! That's why he threw me on the ground.

MARIE: You're dreaming. Because you're not even his type.

HELGA: As if *he* cared about type. He just wants to get it wet.

MARIE: And you're something better, I guess.

HELGA: You're just a slut, that's all.

***

ERICH: Lying there like that, nothin' in his head.

PAUL: We oughta cut off his balls.

ERICH: He really thinks he has it made.

PAUL: That ain't gonna last.

ERICH: That'd be a kick. Just slice off the works. Then he'd see how he could fuck, since he don't think about nothin' else.

PAUL: Besides he stinks like a pig.

ERICH: Bruno said he never washes—

PAUL: Over where he comes from none of them do.

ERICH: Be neat if we had a gun. Make him dance. Imagine him jumpin' for it.

PAUL: But cuttin's better. Give him time to think about it.

ERICH: Then we could soak it in gasoline and give it to Marie for her birthday.

PAUL: Oh that'd be great.

FRANZ: What's Elisabeth sayin' now he's goin' with Marie?

ERICH: She was cryin', because he was real good to her.

PAUL: I believe it because she's a pig. That's for sure.

***

INGRID: The producer said I have a voice as good as Caterina Valente's and I ought to go to Munich for good.

GUNDA: But you need training. *Everyone* can sing.

INGRID: Like you, I suppose.

GUNDA: Just as good as you.

INGRID: We all have our illusions.

GUNDA: And you're somethin' better? A dip. That's what you are. And if anythin's an illusion it's your producer.

INGRID: I'm gonna sing and you're gonna see me on television and then you're gonna be in the shit.

GUNDA: Like your breath.

INGRID: If my breath stinks it's not as bad as you. You're body's rotten it's so old. I'd shut my mouth if I was you. You hear me?

(*Helga.*)

HELGA: Have you heard yet? King Cock, the lousy pig, he nearly beat Erich to death. Went nuts all of a sudden and laid into Erich.

INGRID: Erich. How come?

HELGA: No one knows nothin'. Paul and Franz were there but everything went wild and they just froze.

GUNDA: They didn't help him?

HELGA: Everythin' went wild and they froze.

GUNDA: It was bound to happen. I always said it. "Foreign labor." You got to get rid of it.

INGRID: Right. Foreigners ain't no good.

(*Paul, Erich, Franz.*)

HELGA: So you're here.

INGRID: Can't see many marks from the fight.

ERICH: Because I'm a man who knows the art of self-defense. Otherwise I'd be done in.

PAUL: Right.

ERICH: But he's gonna get some back. Brass knuckles, the crowd and me, we got to beat it out of him.

FRANZ: We'll get a gang together and go after him.

PAUL: Whoever ain't in, is against us and gets it like him.

HELGA: So we get things back to normal—

GUNDA: Plattner's no better.

ERICH: Right. She has to go, because she started it. We're gonna find out what's up, what they think they can do against all of us.

***

HELGA: She even brings him to church. Unbelievable.

GUNDA: Shameless is shameless.

HELGA: He definitely ain't no Christian neither.

GUNDA: Definitely ain't no Christian.

***

ERICH: Fuck him.

GUNDA: Her too.

ERICH: Too bad for Bruno, though. He's mixed up in it, of course.

PAUL: Of course.

***

EVERYONE:
Blood of Christ, quench me
Water from the side of Christ wash me.
Christ's suffering strengthen me
Oh good Jesus hear me
Within thy wounds hide me
Never let me leave thee
So I might ever praise thee
With all thy saints together
For ever and ever amen.

GUNDA: We better tell the priest. Because there ain't no decency in the whole thing.

***

ERICH: I bought some knuckles in Munich.
PAUL: But we oughta keep it quiet.
PAUL: Piss on quiet. Let's do it, the sooner the better.
PAUL: We gotta be careful.

***

FRANZ: Why does she have to bring him with when she goes to church?
MARIE: Because she doesn't know any better. He has religion too.
FRANZ: Yeah, but what kind?
MARIE: What kind don't matter.

***

ELISABETH: You hear what they're saying? All that whispering will mess up the priest's sermon.
BRUNO: I don't hear it.

***

EVERYONE:
The victim is killed,
A lamb in our place;
It's death thou hast willed,
And we witness thy grace.

***

ERICH: You don't get nothin' from nothin'. It's gotta get started.
PAUL: It'd be best in leather jackets, right out in the open. Like they have everywhere except us.
ERICH: That's no reason to wait.

***

GUNDA: I'm gonna talk to her after.
HELGA: Me too.
GUNDA: She'll know what we think of her.

***

MARIE: I'm scared because there ain't nothing good comin' from no one.

FRANZ: Things are just the way they are. You can't change nothin'.

***

EVERYONE:
Our door is marked with blood.
He is our true Paschal lamb
Roast for us in his fierce love.

PAUL, ERICH, FRANZ:
Baa Baa black nigger
Have you any wool?
Yes sir yes sir, three bags full
One for my master, one for my dame
One for the little whore who lives down the lane.

ELISABETH: You referring to me by any chance?

BRUNO: Don't start on them.

ELISABETH: They can do what they want, right?

HELGA: But you can do whatever you want, sure, because you put out in high places.

ELISABETH: Their kind doesn't bother with *you*.

GUNDA: They tried alright, but we got morals. We don't go with everyone.

ELISABETH: "Everyone" beats no one. If I looked like you I'd be ashamed of myself.

GUNDA: You're such a beauty you had to get a foreigner.

ELISABETH: Whose business is that anyhow? Besides, it's not "foreigner"; it's "guest laborer."

HELGA: Not much difference when it's in your bed.

ELISABETH: My bed's my business. Keep your nose out of it.

PAUL, ERICH, FRANZ:
Baa Baa black nigger . . .

ELISABETH: You can see for yourself he's no nigger, and besides he works better than any of you.

ERICH: Are we addressing her?

PAUL: We haven't said a single word to her.

JORGOS: What no understand.

ERICH: You're gonna understand when you swallow your teeth.

JORGOS: No understand.

GUNDA: On account of he upset everything and we want to straighten it out again.

HELGA: We need our peace and quiet.

ELISABETH: Leave me alone and you'll get your peace and quiet.

ERICH: Watch your mouth. If I had a commie in my house . . .

ELISABETH: Get your filthy hands off me.

ERICH: Are my hands dirty? Have a look.

PAUL: Ain't no dirt nowhere.

ERICH: And if they're dirty they ain't no way as dirty as yours.
HELGA: You don't know what shame is.
GUNDA: You pick up whatever's around.
PAUL: And only bother to look at *other* people's dirty wash.
ELISABETH: I'm going. People like you can't be talked to.
ERICH: I oughta beat his head in right now, the commie.
PAUL: Drop it. It's too dangerous.
ERICH: I don't have to take this shit.
PAUL: We'll catch him alone some other time.
MARIE: It won't work then either.
FRANZ: If that's how it has to be.
MARIE: If it wasn't always for the love thing.

***

BRUNO: If everyone's talking there has to be something to it.
ELISABETH: No one knows nothing. Nothing.
BRUNO: What happened happened. That's it.
ELISABETH: And what happened then?
BRUNO: You had a thing goin' with him. That's what happened.
ELISABETH: Nothing happened. Happened! Happened! A load of crap is what I had with him.

***

MARIE: I love you so much, but I have a funny feeling.
JORGOS: Funny feeling.
MARIE: About the others. They're getting ready for something nasty.
JORGOS: No understand.
MARIE: All of a sudden they—bang bang.
JORGOS: No bang bang.
MARIE: Because you're so nice. Still gonna take me to Greece with you?
JORGOS: Go Greece together.
MARIE: And your wife?
JORGOS: No understand.
MARIE: Your wife. Jorgos wife.
JORGOS: No understand.
MARIE: Because it's really got to me. They all know. But it doesn't bother me.

***

INGRID: They're cutting my first record in five weeks because my voice is good enough now.
HELGA: So? How much do you get?
INGRID: I don't know yet. But he's a very nice man. They want my picture too.
HELGA: Then you'll be in the papers.
INGRID: Right. In all the papers. All my savings are sunk into this.
HELGA: You had to pay?
INGRID: Well it's my career.

HELGA: Yea sure.

INGRID: It is! You're only young once, and there are no second chances. Not after.

***

PAUL: I'm for the leather jackets. If you're gonna go for it, go for it.

ERICH: What do they cost? Three hundred.

PAUL: Christ.

ERICH: But there are those American jackets. The blue ones. You could stick somethin' on the back. Chicago Rockers, somethin' like that.

PAUL: Better'n nothin'.

ERICH: And everyone needs a set of knuckles. Got that in your pocket you're flyin'. Bruno's in too. He told me.

PAUL: That's ten of us. Leather jackets would still be better.

***

GUNDA: And then there's marriage. Don't you want to get married?

FRANZ: I don't know.

GUNDA: Married life, now that's somethin'. Don't underestimate the steady life.

FRANZ: You never know.

***

ELISABETH: You been hearing what they say about us?

JORGOS: Jorgos understand all talk.

ELISABETH: But what they say, it's important. You and me. Understand?

JORGOS: Understand.

ELISABETH: Because they all got something for you. But you been with Marie, right?

JORGOS: Marie beautiful girl.

ELISABETH: And me?

JORGOS: Much beautiful.

ELISABETH: So? What about it? With me.

***

ERICH: He threw her in the water.

INGRID: Why in the water?

ERICH: On account of the kid. To get rid of it.

INGRID: Well?

ERICH: Didn't get rid of it. Gave her a shock though.

INGRID: What about Paul?

ERICH: Asked her to forgive him. Now they wanna get married.

INGRID: I wouldn't want to be mixed up in anythin' like that.

ERICH: What about love?

INGRID: That either. Makes you old.

***

MARIE: He tried to kill her.

GUNDA: It was probably just an accident.

MARIE: Ingrid's heading to the city to be a singer.

GUNDA: Because she can sing.

MARIE: Better than us anyhow.

GUNDA: She had to pay for the whole thing though. Even the photographs.

MARIE: Because that's normal.

GUNDA: How do we know what's normal?

\*\*\*

ERICH: You happy with your foreigner?

MARIE: More than with you.

ERICH: Because you're just a slut.

MARIE: If that's what it makes me, I'm happy to be one.

ERICH: God, morals don't mean nothin' to you.

GUNDA: Why do you two have to fight?

ERICH: What's he got that I don't?

MARIE: That's my business.

ERICH: Someone oughta hammer you and your fat mouth.

GUNDA: You shouldn't talk to people the way you do. It gets them riled.

MARIE: I'll talk the way I feel like.

\*\*\*

PAUL: Someone do somethin' to you?

ERICH: No one did anythin' to me, I'm pissed off, that's all.

FRANZ: Well, look who's comin' our way.

PAUL: Yeah, look who's comin' our way. Wa-atch out!

BRUNO: The Greek. Perfect timing.

ERICH: Shitface, hey, what're you doing walkin' over here? You think just anyone can walk over here?

PAUL: Nothin' to say?

JORGOS: No understand.

ERICH: You understand me, commie. Want to hit me back, come over here.

JORGOS: Pustis malakka.

PAUL: Nice one.

ERICH: Just so you don't forget, commie bastard.

JORGOS: Malakka, malakka, ochi!

ERICH: Shut your face, can't you.

JORGOS: Ochi parakalo, ochi!

BRUNO: There's one. There.

ERICH: Just so you don't forget how things are gonna be for you from now on.

\*\*\*

GUNDA: It had to happen sooner or later, they way he carried on here like he
belonged.

HELGA: The way he looked at you like meat in a butcher store.

GUNDA: It won't stop here. Not 'til he's had enough. He's gotta go.

HELGA: Right. We gotta get back to normal.

\*\*\*

INGRID: You were there.

FRANZ: Of course.

INGRID: Is he gonna go?

FRANZ: Who knows. I would, that's for sure.

\*\*\*

PAUL: We had to get revenge.

ERICH: Right.

HELGA: Did he get up again?

ERICH: Dunno. I left.

PAUL: Who cares.

ERICH: Right.

PAUL: He's gonna go for sure.

ERICH: For sure.

HELGA: Because things ain't so nice anymore.

ERICH: We're the only ones who belong here.

\*\*\*

ELISABETH: You didn't have to be in with them. That wasn't necessary.

BRUNO: It just came over me all of a sudden. I don't even know how.

ELISABETH: If you didn't want to help him, ok. But joining in . . .

BRUNO: I didn't want to. I don't know how it happened.

ELISABETH: Sounds like bull to me.

BRUNO: So it's bull.

JORGOS: No understand why.

MARIE: I love you. I'll never leave you.

JORGOS: I no understand why bang-bang.

MARIE: Ok it's over now. Settle down.

JORGOS: All, all, bang-bang.

MARIE: Hold me. Come on.

JORGOS: All, me, bang-bang.

MAIRE: Give me a kiss. Be nice.

JORGOS: I no understand. Greece nice. Germany much cold.

MARIE: Kiss me. I need you.

\*\*\*

GUNDA: So? Is he going?

BRUNO: No.

PAUL: And did you tell Elisabeth she won't get off any better next time?

BRUNO: Yeah, but she doesn't believe it.

ERICH: She's crazy.

HELGA: It's easy to see what's better for her.

BRUNO: She says it's better for business.

ERICH: If he stays.

BRUNO: Right, because it's true.

GUNDA: How come?

BRUNO: Because we produce more now, and she only pays him six hundred fifty marks. He sleeps in my room and she deducts a hundred fifty marks for that.

GUNDA: A hundred fifty. That's allowed?

BRUNO: Right. And for food another hundred eighty. That comes to three hundred thirty marks. She pays him three hundred twenty marks.

ERICH: Not bad.

BRUNO: That's what the man from the foreign labor department in Munich told her. You have to do it that way because then it's more productive because they're here and the money stays in the country.

ERICH: So that's how it is.

BRUNO: Right. It's a trick. For Germany's sake.

HELGA: She knows about business, that Elisabeth. I always said so.

BRUNO: And she's not gonna ship anyone out, she told me. More likely she'll get another one.

PAUL: You need savvy, that's what it takes.

***

GUNDA: She had a miscarriage. But they want to get married anyway.

INGRID: Don't mean nothin' to me. Miscarriage, marriage.

GUNDA: Even if your career don't work out?

INGRID: Maybe. When I get old. Nothin' doin'.

***

ELISABETH: I had to talk to him for hours to get him to stay.

BRUNO: I can't help it.

ELISABETH: If he tells them in Munich what happened here they won't send any more.

BRUNO: I can't help it. No way.

ELISABETH: If it happens again I kick you out.

BRUNO: I can't help it.

ELISABETH: And I'm gonna make a report because that's no way to act.

BRUNO: I didn't do nothin'.

***

ERICH: So in March I'm joinin' the Army. Because it beats workin' here.

PAUL: I'm gonna have to too.

ERICH: That's for me. I want to be in a submarine because it's different. From bein' on land I mean.

PAUL: You have to go where they tell you.

ERICH: Who cares where you go anyway.

***

ELISABETH: You'll be having a colleague in January. A Turk. He's too old for construction or something.

JORGOS: Turkish?

ELISABETH: A Turk's coming here. Work like you.

JORGOS: Turkish no good. Others no?

ELISABETH: No, because I have to take what they send me.

JORGOS: Turkish no. Jorgos and Turkish no work together. Jorgos go to other town.

***

MARIE: He's taking me to Greece with him in the summer.

HELGA: What about his wife?

MARIE: It doesn't make any difference. It's not the same in Greece.

HELGA: I don't know. Just goin' away like that. And so far too.

END

# Blood on the Cat's Neck

CHARACTERS:

Phoebe Zeitgeist
The Girl
The Model
The Mistress
The Dead Soldier's Wife
The Butcher
The Lover
The Teacher
The Soldier
The Policeman

*Setting as in a boulevard play. Phoebe Zeitgeist sits motionless in an armchair, etc. We hear a man's voice over a loudspeaker: "Phoebe Zeitgeist has been sent to the earth from a distant star to write an eyewitness account of human democracy. But Phoebe Zeitgeist has difficulty, because although she has learned the words, she doesn't understand human language."*

## POLICEMAN + PHOEBE

POLICEMAN: What's your name? I asked your name. Christ, are you good look-ing. You got some ID? My aunt, she's retarded. Got a hole in her head. I mean really nuts. Look honey, I need the details—so I can book it and let you go. Otherwise—you get the electric chair. (*He laughs.*) Is your name . . . Maria? Magdalena? Marion? Marina? Shit! Everyone has ID. People who don't have ID, I learned this, they don't exist. Open your yap you silly cunt or I'll smack you. Ok. That's called obstruction. That pisses me off. Ok. It's nature's law, sort of, I know. But . . . the laws I have to obey, you don't find that in nature, they're in books. I open to a page and I read: "vagrancy," for instance . . . or . . . wait a minute, but you look real intelligent. That's a designer dress. You're clean, well groomed. You ought to know your name.

***

## BUTCHER

BUTCHER: I liked this girl a lot. She was real young and had black hair. Friday night I'd pick her up and we'd go for a walk or to the movies. Then I wasn't lonely anymore. I liked working the whole week because I figured on Friday I'm not going to be alone anymore. My first boss used to hit me, when I was eighteen years old. Day-dreaming used to help, or just thinking about her. Then one Friday she didn't come out. I went back home. "She must be sick," I thought, "or busy." But she didn't come out at all on Fridays anymore, and I cried. From that moment on I couldn't love another girl. Now every Friday I go out and buy myself a girl. A few times I tried paying for a little talk. But whores don't like to talk much because they just think about the money and getting it over with. Now I'm the butcher and I have a kid working for me who gets hit when he deserves it. I really yearn for a little love.

***

## LOVER + PHOEBE

LOVER: You hands are so soft. Look into my eyes. (*He turns her face towards him.*) You have the eyes of a married woman. I like married women. They appreciate tenderness. The younger ones—you know how it is—they *expect* it. Then they want something different. But that's about all a man who knows and understands women can offer. Right here is the most precious part of a human being—the chalice at the joint of the upper and lower arm. (*He kisses her.*) Do you enjoy my touch? I'm sure you do. And married women are so quiet, so reserved. You may rest assured that age isn't a problem. I had a lover who was going on sixty. But—older, wearier flesh can respond passionately to a lover's familiar touch. I love you. I love your forehead, here at the hairline. You are precious. You glow as a lily in twilight, dear one. I will make you happy. I will explore every part of your body. You will come to know your own skin through my touch. The feeling will never leave you.

***

## SOLDIER

SOLDIER: Mother knew best, always. No matter what I asked, she'd answer me. I'd come home and say, "Mama, heat up some soup." I didn't have to wait long. Or bread and butter, sprinkled with sugar. Or soft-boiled eggs in a cup when I was sick. She had a good handle on her child. She told me how to get on in the world so I wouldn't get into trouble, stuff like that. It was good advice. In almost every situation I could tell how far to go, and I could see what people wanted out of me. When things got bad in the war, and everyone was crammed into the trenches, trembling and with tears in their eyes, I kept the image of my mother in mind. She was telling me not to despair. I'm looking for a girl who can be what my mother was for me. I can't find her.

***

## TEACHER + PHOEBE

TEACHER: Take a poem or a single line.

"Over all the mountaintops quiet reigns,
In the deep green forests not a breath stirs,
Birds go silent,
And you,
Just wait,
Soon you too will come to rest."

Do you take my meaning? The poet can say things which far outstrip the realm of the normally utterable. The poet is capable of feeling moods which have not yet materialized. And—the poet already *knows* things before ordinary mortals have their first inkling. That is why we must learn to analyze the poet and his work. This applies to me as well. And it is the express function of our schools. Of course we must also study profane subjects like the simple times tables, or geography and biology. No question. But nothing is of greater siginificance than understanding our poets and thinkers. I'm also aware that business deals and balance sheets make up most of human existence. For that very reason people need diversion. Then afterwards they're better equipped to fill their slots in life. I am sure ours will be a shared learning experience.

***

## WIFE OF THE DEAD SOLDIER

WIFE: If my husband were still alive he'd be making about fifteen hundred marks a month. My husband was a locksmith. The state now pays me three hundred and forty marks a month for him as a war casualty. Fifteen hundred for three is however more than three hundred and forty for two. But no one seems to grasp that. They figured out for me how someone can survive on three hundred and forty marks. Twenty percent they figure for an apartment. That comes to seventy marks. You're allowed eighty-five marks a person for staple foods, which comes to one hundred and seventy marks for me and my daughter. Clothes and laundry for two gives you fifty marks. And school supplies for my daughter are worth twenty marks. They said the three hundred and ten marks that comes to, leaves thirty for luxury items, like chocolate, cigarettes, movies, alcohol, radio, books, gifts, vacations. The people who worked all this out for me were very friendly.

***

## GIRL + PHOEBE

GIRL: Of course, first of all you have to know what you want. If you want to study to be a typist that's simple. Or a stenographer! Of course you also have the option of finding a man to marry. In fact, *everyone* tries that. Anyhow, it's really good to have a profession to fall back on. A profession can spell freedom, you know. But of course you still have to be adaptable. No way around that. Adapt! Which doesn't mean you have to think differently than you really do, right away anyhow. To start, though, you have to repress your own thoughts. It's the same with your dreams and desires. You know you can really get along in this society, it really has something to offer. You just need to know when to hold back. You can't have everything of course. That'd be too much anyway. Basically, you're responsible for all of it. If you lift your hand it's your responsibility. Or if you speak, it's your responsibility. You're responsible for everything.

\*\*\*

## MODEL

MODEL: I lie in bed and fondle myself. Often. There's never been anyone else who could do it just the right way. So I do it myself—simple. I have a great deal of contact with men in my profession, and I sleep with a lot of them. That's no problem for me. And why should it be? It's never really mattered, just something that happens, like drinking a cup of coffee, or the rain falling. It could be that other people frighten me. Because relationships are very demanding. Don't you think? When someone takes a photo of me it's wonderful. For me it is a sensual experience to pose for a few moments, or to smile. Even when I'm alone. There's this soft down on my stomach, and on my thigh, very soft, on the inner part. And my shoulders have muscles, so . . . I like myself a lot. I won't really let anyone else get in the way.

\*\*\*

## LOVER + PHOEBE

LOVER: Submission is beautiful. People can learn to enjoy it. There are books, you should read them, where women turn into complete females. They exist for the sole purpose of giving pleasure to the men they love. Of course it's obscene. Blindfolded, and chained or tied up—to let yourself be whipped. For women, happiness is submission. You will learn this, dear, and understand it. You will learn to throw yourself down and be ready when the man you love looks at you. And when he shows contempt, you are to kiss his feet in gratitude, because you have been privileged to know what it means to be used by him. And, my dear, do not use your brain for thinking. Your brain exists—for hoping, with him, that he will want you. Your brain exists to achieve the frenzy which will make you happy. The man is everything; you are nothing.

\*\*\*

## THE MISTRESS

THE MISTRESS: I lived quite a while with a couple of women. It was a commune, sort of. A group of women who talked things over and tried to work out where the oppression of women in our society comes from, how it originates. Questions we wanted to answer for example were why marriage is so much more deeply embedded in women's consciousness than in men's, stuff like that. We had decided to treat men just the way we thought they treated us. We tried to swap roles. Of course that's ridiculous, even repressive. It didn't lead to anything in the end. In the end all the bullshit leads us to enjoy having an oppressed consciousness. Society is not going to let itself change like that.

***

## MODEL + PHOEBE

MODEL: I'm afraid of getting old. What would be the point in being alive? We all need to have fun. The way you get it's your own thing. You have a nice figure. Really. You should have some options and believe me, that's the most important thing. How will I be able to tell I'm still alive? When no one cares about me? Then who will I be? No one! I have a friend. She was a top model, the best, really, and now she's forty-two and washed up. The whole day she spends in her apartment staring at the telephone. And there's not a single bastard who will call her up. That's exactly how it'd be with me, I know, except I won't let it because I'll kill myself first. A life of despair? Forget it. You just need to make sure you bail out in time. But I can't tell you how. Maybe with a husband, children. Or some bright idea to help you get it together. Or death. Maybe death's best after all.

***

## GIRL

GIRL: My father used to hit me. A lot. And always on my naked butt. He liked it I guess. Back then I thought almost everything was unfair, but now I can understand how it was. Why he hit me and all, I guess. But anyhow he didn't have to enjoy it. That sure was rotten. I had a boyfriend who used to comb his hair sort of like Elvis Presley. I thought that was really neat. To me Elvis Presley was the greatest. Actually he was for all of us in those days. It makes me cry when I put the records on, the way it reminds me of those days and how everything was. It sure was nice, and ain't no one going to give it back to you. What's gone is gone. And sometimes too when I walk down a street a smell will remind me of the past, or of a house, and I remember how it felt when I lived in the old apartment house where me and my friends were all together and I wasn't alone. "What's past is past," my mother always used to say. She got it right with a lot of the things she used to say.

***

## WIFE OF THE DEAD SOLDIER + PHOEBE

WIFE: Then one day the letter came. It was blue and I knew right away what was in it because by that time I hadn't heard a word from my husband for four weeks. I couldn't read it because things went all blurry. Somehow I knew it even before it happened. I suddenly got this feeling, "Franz—he's dead now," and it was like I was being strangled. People are always talking about this sort of thing, and you don't believe them, but when it happens—funny.

Strangled, not able to get any more air. But take it from me, people can endure a lot. You can endure a lot even when you think beforehand you'd never be able to stand it. When it happens, life carries on even if something inside you has been snuffed out. I always say it, suffering is a part of life too. That's how it is. Sure you can try to avoid it, but sooner or later you'll realize it was pointless. You *can't* avoid it! All that wasted energy. You could have put it to better use.

***

## TEACHER

TEACHER: It took a long time for me to admit to myself that I like men better than women. Much too long. But I was just afraid of the consequences. I thought I'd have to live underground—toilets, bus depots, that kind of thing. It's frightening if you've had a normal upbringing. You shy away from it. But as a matter of fact it's completely different. My boyfriend is a dancer from Guinea, and we live like man and wife. All perfectly regular. We have fun, visit friends. Everything in life depends on how you go about it. There was a time when I was always on the prowl, looking for it almost every night. But I figure that's how it is with straights too until they find a steady partner.

***

## SOLDIER + PHOEBE

SOLDIER: I have the hots for you, sister. Ever done it with a soldier? Soldiers are better than other men because every fuck's the last fuck. Don't play coy, honey, come on. You *are* a woman, aren't you? Sure you are. And women don't think about anything but men. That's how it is. Hey, right, fight back. I go for that. I want a con-quest. Broads who just lie back and spread, I don't want none of that. Doesn't turn me on. Hey, honey, let's hear you scream. I'll stuff it in your mouth. Don't be so boring. Jesus Christ, these refined cunts! You need to go begging half a dozen times before they come across like they should. Hey, you know, you *are* real hot. Some legs, ooh. Wild. Belly, nice tits. Groove it, girl, I'm a man. I need the girl to react so I can tell I'm doing it good. Come on.

***

## LOVER

LOVER: I've already tried a lot—jobs, professional training. I'm not cut out for work. I use women now instead. And I'm always ready to return the favor. It got started with one who hadn't had any for a long time. She really thought she was past it. Was she grateful! We both made out. I made some cash and the woman got herself a little taste of tenderness. You know. I don't think I have anything to be ashamed of. The women get more out of it than I do.

Otherwise no one would even look at them anymore. And me, I could make money somewhere else. It doesn't matter. And anyhow they're all so thankful it's impossible to say anything bad about it. Sometimes I even think I actually prefer the older ones. Those young girls they scare me, really. I really get scared. Honest. I guess we all find our niche.

*** 

## BUTCHER + PHOEBE

BUTCHER: If you have a shop you buy meat in the morning for example. Let's say a thousand marks worth, and you cut it and sell it by closing time. But you can't cut the meat on your own. It'd be too much for you. If you're on your own you can cut and sell two hundred marks worth of meat, so you hire four shop assistants who allow you to re-sell the meat—the meat you got for a thousand—to re-sell it for five thousand. So you have a turnover of five thousand. To make that much you have to pay the help two hundred marks apiece, a total of eight hundred marks. OK, so you buy the meat for a thousand marks, eight hundred goes for help and two hundred rent, a total of a thousand for expenses. That leaves you three thousand profit. If you were on your own you'd clear six hundred maximum, which is to say that each employee makes you eight hundred marks. So for each two hundred marks he earns from you, you earn eight hundred from him. It's that simple.

*** 

## POLICEMAN

POLICEMAN: I have an uncle who was a cop. Right after the war. Blackmarket everywhere. One day they caught him dealing in cigarettes—he wanted to make some money for his family. He had to leave the force. After a time he bought a cart and became a street vendor, sold fruit. He'd go up and down the lanes between the houses yelling out "strawberries, fresh strawberries." And then he got married. His wife used to help him, and then he started drinking. And every time he got stewed he used to start crying and sobbing because he wasn't a cop anymore and because being a cop was really something special. Then he got sick. And loved his wife very much. They decided to open up a store when he got better, a genuine business. So he's pretty happy there now on account of he has a shop assistant who helps him. And I became a cop.

*** 

LOVER: Your mother's a bitch.
POLICEMAN: You talking to me?
LOVER: Straight up and down: a bitch.
POLICEMAN: Get over here.
LOVER: You got a problem?
POLICEMAN: Or I'll go over to you.

LOVER: Try it.

POLICEMAN: Ok. What did you just say?

LOVER: Nothing.

POLICEMAN: Chicken shit. Got your tail between your legs now, huh? You think I'm deaf?

LOVER: Ow.

POLICEMAN: Go ahead and yell. First you shoot off your mouth, you bastard, then you turn chicken. My mother don't belong anywhere in your mouth. Nowhere. You got that?

LOVER: Yeah.

POLICEMAN: Then get it.

LOVER: Fucking sadistic pig. I'll show you.

POLICEMAN: You ain't showing me nothing.

PHOEBE: YOUR MOTHER IS A BITCH.

GIRL: Please no. Don't tell the cops. I already said I was sorry.

TEACHER: Thief today, killer tomorrow.

GIRL: My parents can't find this out.

TEACHER: Special consideration? Why? This girl was caught stealing.

GIRL: Please, please don't. I'm so ashamed of myself.

TEACHER: You should have thought of that before. After, no one's going to believe you.

GIRL: My father's been sick for two years. Things are rough at home. Please.

TEACHER: It's always the same with you criminals. Work-shy, then tears afterwards. We're going to the police.

GIRL: NO! No, no, no, no! My father's dying. He's sick.

TEACHER: What should I care about your domestic problems?

GIRL: Have pity, please.

TEACHER: No chance. For me justice is what matters.

PHOEBE: THIEF TODAY, KILLER TOMORROW. WHAT SHOULD I CARE ABOUT YOUR DOMESTIC PROBLEMS? FOR ME JUSTICE IS WHAT MATTERS.

TEACHER: How much you make a day?

LOVER: Hundred, two hundred. Depends.

TEACHER: You're very attractive.

LOVER: I know. That's what they all say.

TEACHER: Well, la-dee-da!

LOVER: I'm sorry. I didn't mean to offend you.

TEACHER: No. Do you do it with the ladies too?

LOVER: Sometimes. Not very often.

TEACHER: Why?

LOVER: Oh, it just happens. In the beginning I needed the balance. Time cures that. You get used to everything.

TEACHER: Don't you like it?

LOVER: What? With men?

TEACHER: Yeah.

LOVER: For cash? Doesn't bother me one way or the other.

TEACHER: And compassion? Don't you have the slightest sense of compassion?

LOVER: I try to keep out of that. I don't want to get involved in too much.

TEACHER: Why? That's part of life too.

LOVER: I'm afraid.

PHOEBE: YOU GET USED TO EVERYTHING. I DON'T WANT TO GET INVOLVED IN TOO MUCH. I'M AFRAID.

GIRL: Did you go to college?

THE MISTRESS: Yes. But I quit. You?

GIRL: No. We didn't have enough money.

THE MISTRESS: It's not a question of money.

GIRL: I had to make a living. That's a fact.

THE MISTRESS: You wanted to be a pediatrician, didn't you?

GIRL: People change their minds.

THE MISTRESS: That's true. But you seem . . . fatigued. You even wanted to go to Africa in those days. You had ideals.

GIRL: They burned themselves out.

THE MISTRESS: All your ideals? Gone?

GIRL: Yes. You're right. I am fatigued. People get that way. What are you up to?

THE MISTRESS: Not much. I have a business. Runs itself. I inherited enough to get started, and now I'm grinding along.

GIRL: That's not what you wanted to do when you were young either.

THE MISTRESS: No.

PHOEBE: THAT'S A FACT. PEOPLE CHANGE THEIR MINDS. I AM FATIGUED.

DEAD SOLDIER'S WIFE: How do you get your figure like that?

MODEL: I take care of myself.

DEAD SOLDIER'S WIFE: There's more to it than care. Me, I have to work. That ages your hands, makes them brittle.

MODEL: I'm sorry but I work too.

DEAD SOLDIER'S WIFE: Things turned out better for you. It's ok that there are differences in the world. That's how it is.

MODEL: I like my work. Maybe that's why . . .

DEAD SOLDIER'S WIFE: But not everyone can enjoy their work. You should be grateful.

MODEL: I don't talk about it so much either, like you.

DEAD SOLDIER'S WIFE: When you're unhappy, you have to talk about it. There's nothing else left. I learned that much. No one's going to take that away.

PHOEBE: IT'S OK THAT THERE ARE DIFFERENCES IN THE WORLD. THAT'S HOW IT IS. WHEN YOU'RE UNHAPPY, YOU HAVE TO TALK ABOUT IT.

POLICEMAN: It starts to get light around six, then it begins.

TEACHER: Ever had a premonition? Anything like that?

POLICEMAN: A premonition of what?

TEACHER: Death for example. Or the end.

POLICEMAN: No. Why?

TEACHER: I sense something. Something's going to happen tomorrow. I feel it in my gut. It's a feeling I can't put into words.

POLICEMAN: Then keep it to yourself. That kind of talk can scare people.

TEACHER: But I have to talk. I have to confront my thoughts, or they eat away at me. Maybe death's really beautiful. Peace and quiet.

POLICEMAN: Cut it out! I don't want to die yet. You understand? Shut your stupid fucking mouth, you bastard. (Cries.)

TEACHER: We're all afraid.

PHOEBE: A PREMONITION OF THE END. I HAVE TO CONFRONT MY THOUGHTS. I DON'T WANT TO DIE. WE'RE ALL AFRAID.

GIRL: You can't leave, just like that. There's still something between us. It can't end so fast.

LOVER: Look at yourself. You're nuts. It's written all over your face.

GIRL: Because I love you.

LOVER: Beat it.

GIRL: Franz! If you leave, I'm going to kill myself.

LOVER: Who cares? That doesn't bother me.

GIRL: You can't be that rotten. You cared for me once.

LOVER: It's over. Anyone can tell that.

GIRL: It's not over. I need you Franz. You can't leave.

LOVER: You'll see what I can do. You make me want to puke.

GIRL: You're rotten, really rotten. You don't deserve to have another happy day in your life.

LOVER: Time will tell.

PHOEBE: THERE'S STILL SOMETHING BETWEEN US. WHO CARES? I NEED YOU. YOU MAKE ME WANT TO PUKE.

TEACHER: Is your son doing better in school now?

THE MISTRESS: Oh, a little. We pampered him when he was younger. That leaves its mark.

TEACHER: Of course. Forget about what people say, to me a strict upbringing is the best introduction to life.

THE MISTRESS: That may well be true.

TEACHER: No question. Does life do any "pampering?" Exactly. I use cheap shots on my son to prepare him for the cheap shots he can expect from life.

THE MISTRESS: Do you hit your son a lot?

TEACHER: What's "a lot" supposed to mean? I'd say, as often as necessary. Children need corporal punishment and they let you know exactly when. I just follow the dictates of my reason.

PHOEBE: PAMPERING LEAVES ITS MARK. A STRICT UPBRINGING IS THE BEST INTRODUCTION TO LIFE.

SOLDIER: How much?

MODEL: A hundred.

SOLDIER: How much!

MODEL: One hun-dred.

SOLDIER: Are you nuts? A hundred, on Friday?

MODEL: Not much Friday action 'is time.

SOLDIER: Why'd you come home so early then?

MODEL: My feet hurt, Max.

SOLDIER: I wanted to rent a car and go for a drive tomorrow. A hundred marks won't even pay for a lousy meal.

MODEL: Don't yell like that, please. Wasn't no action and my feet hurt . . . I'm sorry.

SOLDIER: Look honey-pie, I'm not gonna put up with that, you understand. Pack your things and get out of here. Understand?

MODEL: Max, I . . .

SOLDIER: Understand?

MODEL: I'm going.

PHOEBE: ARE YOU NUTS? MY FEET HURT. PACK YOUR THINGS.

SOLDIER: Next year we can go on another vacation. But now we have to save.

DEAD SOLDIER'S WIFE: Yes.

SOLDIER: You don't need to make such a sour face. You get something out of it too.

DEAD SOLDIER'S WIFE: I never said a word.

SOLDIER: I know your tricks, the way you pull a face when you say something. The debts are there, that's all. No one's going to make them disappear.

DEAD SOLDIER'S WIFE: That much I know.

SOLDIER: Bullshit's what you know. You don't have to go to work. You just rake in the goodies.

DEAD SOLDIER'S WIFE: Now stop it, please.

SOLDIER: I ain't gonna stop. No one takes nothing away from me. No bitch anyhow.

DEAD SOLDIER'S WIFE: Whatever you say.

SOLDIER: Yeah, you can stick with me, sure, long as it don't cost you nothing.

DEAD SOLDIER'S WIFE: I love you.

PHOEBE: YOU DON'T HAVE TO GO TO WORK. YOU JUST RAKE IN THE GOODIES. NO ONE TAKES NOTHING AWAY FROM ME. I LOVE YOU.

POLICEMAN: I love you.

GIRL: Yeah.

POLICEMAN: I could never hurt you. Never.

GIRL: What makes you think of that?

POLICEMAN: Everyone hurts me.

GIRL: Yeah?

POLICEMAN: Yeah.

GIRL: I'm still young. I don't know nothing.

POLICEMAN: You'll learn. You're beautiful. I don't want to hurt you.

GIRL: Don't keep saying that. It depresses me.

POLICEMAN: I don't want you to be depressed. But I'm warning you. Someone who's nice, he can be nasty too. That's a fact. You're so young.

GIRL: Yeah.

POLICEMAN: Pain is the price you pay. No one gets off scot free.

GIRL: The way you're holding me now is beautiful. I wish it could last forever.

POLICEMAN: Beautiful things never last long.

PHOEBE: WE ALL HURT EACH OTHER. YOU ARE BEAUTIFUL. IT DE-PRESSES ME. PAIN IS THE PRICE YOU PAY. BEAUTIFUL THINGS NEVER LAST LONG.

THE MISTRESS: I always feel sick afterwards. Kiss me. You're so good.

LOVER: I know. You're good too.

THE MISTRESS: Yeah. Will we be seeing each other again?

LOVER: No.

THE MISTRESS: Too bad. I'd have liked that.

LOVER: I can't do it twice with the same person. It starts to get serious and I can't stand it. I don't want to be glued to another human being.

THE MISTRESS: That sounds rotten when you've just done it with someone, especially when it was good.

LOVER: When a relationship begins to form I can't breathe. I have to be careful.

THE MISTRESS: Then when it *does* form, you're stuck.

LOVER: Not me. You can count on it.

THE MISTRESS: Plenty have said that before you, and they got caught anyway. Nature's law.

PHOEBE: KISS ME. YOU'RE SO GOOD. I DON'T WANT TO BE GLUED TO ANOTHER HUMAN BEING. THAT SOUNDS ROTTEN. I HAVE TO BE CAREFUL. NATURE'S LAW.

TEACHER: You are going to die.

MODEL: How do you know?

TEACHER: Your eyes. There's death in your eyes.

MODEL: Liar!

TEACHER: I don't need to lie.

MODEL: Why do you want to torture me like this?

TEACHER: If I *did* want to . . . I'd probably get a kick out of it.

MODEL: You're rotten.

TEACHER: Death comes quick. You'll die in bed. First you'll feel a little sick, then you'll sense something's wrong, then fear will set in. Overwhelming fear. You will feel pity for yourself..

MODEL: Stop it. Stop it! I can't stand to listen. I've always been petrified of dying.

TEACHER: I was just fooling. Honest.

MODEL: Lot of help that does me. I'm never going to get over this.

PHOEBE: YOU ARE GOING TO DIE. LIAR! YOU'RE ROTTEN. YOU WILL FEEL PITY FOR YOURSELF. STOP IT!

GIRL: Is your husband still making as little as he used to?

MODEL: Little?!

GIRL: Yeah, well, if that's not little I don't know what is.

MODEL: A little or a lot, we survive.

GIRL: As if surviving was enough. You have to be able to take care of yourself.

MODEL: We're in love.

GIRL: Come off it. How come there's always so much yelling in your place then?

MODEL: Are you trying to start something?

GIRL: Me? What are you getting at?

MODEL: Looks that way. The way you're talking.

GIRL: I talk how I talk. I say what comes to me. That is apparently *not* the way you operate.

MODEL: You're just jealous.

GIRL: Jealous? Of you, maybe? That's too much.

MODEL: Of course you are, don't even have a husband yet.

GIRL: Correct. But I wouldn't look twice at the one you've got.

PHOEBE: YOU HAVE TO BE ABLE TO TAKE CARE OF YOURSELF. ARE YOU TRYING TO START SOMETHING? YOU'RE JUST JEALOUS.

DEAD SOLDIER'S WIFE: I want my husband back. You took my husband.

THE MISTRESS: He *belongs* to you?

DEAD SOLDIER'S WIFE: Before the eyes of God . . . and man.

THE MISTRESS: Poor little thing. Who believes in eternity these days?

DEAD SOLDIER'S WIFE: Me.

THE MISTRESS: Come. Sit down next to me. He just has more fun with me than with you. He couldn't have known that before.

DEAD SOLDIER'S WIFE: But that's just not true.

THE MISTRESS: Ask him. If he's honest he'll tell you. I'm better in bed, no question.

DEAD SOLDIER'S WIFE: God, oh God are you rotten.

THE MISTRESS: I'm not rotten, darling, just honest.

DEAD SOLDIER'S WIFE: Set him free. Without that man I am so lonely.

LOVED ONE: It's his affair. His choice. I have no control over it.

PHOEBE: WHO BELIEVES IN ETERNITY THESE DAYS? I'M JUST HONEST.

MODEL: You may lick my feet, dog!

BUTCHER: Woof, woof.

MODEL: That's a good little puppy, nice. Yes like that. Get off, you mangy shit. (*Butcher howls.*) You stink.

BUTCHER: Don't tell me I stink, please.

MODEL: On your knees! Bark! Or should I get the whip?

BUTCHER: Woof, woof.

MODEL: Yes, very nice. You'll know who I am, you mangy shit.

BUTCHER: I've had enough for today. Can I get up?

MODEL: Sure. But leave me alone.

BUTCHER: You always treat me so badly.

PHOEBE: YOU MAY LICK MY FEET. GET OFF, YOU MANGY SHIT. YOU ALWAYS TREAT ME SO BADLY.

POLICEMAN: A motorcycle, hey that's wild. Love and death and time whizzing by all at once. The greatest.

THE MISTRESS: Give me a ride.

POLICEMAN: You're too old. Honest.

THE MISTRESS: Too old?

POLICEMAN: Of course. I mean you're neat . . . to screw and all. But the motorcycle thing, that's different.

THE MISTRESS: Do all men differentiate like that?

POLICEMAN: I got no clue how it is with anyone else. You're too refined. You on a motorcycle! They'd laugh in my face.

THE MISTRESS: And that's so bad?

POLICEMAN: Bad? The absolute worst. When someone makes fun of me I go nuts. You understand? I stop at nothing. (*The Mistress laughs.*) Quit laughing, you hear? Or I'll wring your neck, you hear? You won't see me soon again, you bitch.

PHOEBE: WHEN SOMEONE MAKES FUN OF ME I GO NUTS. YOU UNDERSTAND?

MODEL: By the way, I fired the maid.

LOVER: You fired . . .?

MODEL: Yes.

LOVER: And . . .?

MODEL: You mean why? It was too much for me. The whole city was talking about you. I'm embarrassed.

LOVER: But we worked out an arrangement for this marriage, you and I.

MODEL: So?

LOVER: Agreements exist so both parties will respect their conditions, no? We didn't want to cramp each other.

MODEL: I had no way of knowing that when it came to it I couldn't stand the freedom.

LOVER: But I need to be free, you understand. I like the girl.

MODEL: I couldn't have taken it anymore.

PHOEBE: I'M EMBARRASSED. WE DIDN'T WANT TO CRAMP EACH

OTHER. I NEED TO BE FREE. I COULDN'T HAVE TAKEN IT ANYMORE.

TEACHER: You keep the child. That's plenty.

DEAD SOLDIER'S WIFE: Where am I supposed to live with the child? Huh? I need the house, Peter. I have to have it.

TEACHER: Don't be ridiculous, gramma. What do you think I've been working for for twenty years?

DEAD SOLDIER'S WIFE: Stop being so rotten. We were supposed to talk this over calmly.

TEACHER: I can't stay calm. You always wanted to use me. Always.

DEAD SOLDIER'S WIFE: That's just not true, Peter. Just think about it. We *both* saved for the house.

TEACHER: But I had to work. Not you.

DEAD SOLDIER'S WIFE: I don't even want it for myself. I'm just thinking of the child.

TEACHER: The child never loved me. Shit, I'm not going to let myself be sucked in by you again. I'm through. I keep the house. Basta.

DEAD SOLDIER'S WIFE: Then we have to go to court. You want that?

TEACHER: Yes.

PHOEBE: YOU ALWAYS WANTED TO USE ME. THE CHILD NEVER LOVED ME.

THE MISTRESS: Maybe you're just a lazy bastard. The way you hang around in bed all day.

SOLDIER: So? I'm sick.

THE MISTRESS: You bet you're sick. We're all sick.

SOLDIER: Come here.

THE MISTRESS: No.

SOLDIER: He-ey. Come here.

THE MISTRESS: I mean it. I break my back all day and you hang out in bed. And at night you hit the booze, without me.

SOLDIER: But we're always together anyhow.

THE MISTRESS: Yeah? When? One hour—when I cook your supper. And I love being with you so much.

SOLDIER: I know. Without me you don't exist..

THE MISTRESS: So? I have a hard time being alone.

SOLDIER: Nothing to be ashamed of there. No one can stand it alone for very long. That's human. But there's more to life than your woman—who you always have to be with, always.

PHOEBE: I LOVE BEING WITH YOU SO MUCH. NO ONE CAN STAND IT ALONE FOR VERY LONG.

DEAD SOLDIER'S WIFE: You hit me. You almost beat me to death.

BUTCHER: Shut your face. You want the whole house to hear.

DEAD SOLDIER'S WIFE: Yes, yes, yes. You hit me. He beat me!!!

BUTCHER: Shut up or I will kill you, you hear me? Maria, please.

DEAD SOLDIER'S WIFE: Don't touch me.

BUTCHER: Be nice. I'm sorry.

DEAD SOLDIER'S WIFE: Help, help!

BUTCHER: Be quiet. Or I'll make you be quiet.

DEAD SOLDIER'S WIFE: He's killing me. Help.

BUTCHER: Maria, please! Please. Please, please.

DEAD SOLIDER'S WIFE: No . . . You . . . No! . . . Stop . . .

BUTCHER: I can't hear you yelling anymore. I can't. I told you I was sorry. Maria . . . Maria . . . Listen to me . . . Maria . . . My God . . . Maria!!! I didn't want that to happen. I didn't want it to happen. Honest. Our father who art in heaven. Forgive me.

PHOEBE: DON'T TOUCH ME. I DIDN'T WANT THAT TO HAPPEN. OUR FATHER WHO ART IN HEAVEN, FORGIVE ME.

MODEL: Of course my husband doesn't know anything about me. We never talk.

POLICEMAN: Cigarette?

MODEL: Yes. Thank you. We live in different worlds.

POLICEMAN: But at one time there must have been something. Between a him and a her.

MODEL: Sex? Of course. I was so young then. But that's ancient history.

POLICEMAN: I think you're beautiful.

MODEL: Thank you. I like to hear that. Like all women. Right?

POLICEMAN: I mean this seriously. I have known very few women who were as . . . as, pardon me, but as perfect as you. I adore you, Laura.

MODEL: I like you. We could . . .

POLICEMAN: Yes?

MODEL: We . . . I . . . I'd like to sleep with you.

POLICEMAN: I know. I'd be good.

MODEL: Yes. I'm sure.

PHOEBE: I THINK YOU'RE BEAUTIFUL. I ADORE YOU. I'D LIKE TO SLEEP WITH YOU.

LOVER: We can't take care of a kid. You know that as well as I do.

DEAD SOLDIER'S WIFE: Yes.

LOVER: Good. So we don't need to talk about it. It's obvious.

DEAD SOLDIER'S WIFE: But I don't want to get rid of it. I want to keep it. I'll even starve for it. I already love it—a lot.

LOVER: That's you. I'm not going to arrange my life around something like that. There are enough other important things in the world.

DEAD SOLDIER'S WIFE: A child is yours, really yours. It'd stick with you. Not like other people.

LOVER: But I'm not leaving you.

DEAD SOLDIER'S WIFE: People say that kind of thing, and later they change their minds. Then you're alone.

LOVER: If you don't trust me, every minute I spend with you is one minute too many.

DEAD SOLDIER'S WIFE: Karl!

PHOEBE: A CHILD IS YOURS, REALLY YOURS. WITHOUT TRUST IT'S ALL TOO MUCH TO BEAR.

SOLDIER: Beer! I'll break his fucking head. One more sound, and "whack."

TEACHER: Cut it out. There's no use.

SOLDIER: Oh yeah there is. Jesus God am I stewed.

TEACHER: Right.

SOLDIER: Who gives a fuck? I do what I want when I'm drunk. More than when I'm sober too. Sober, who cares?

TEACHER: He didn't do anything to you, did he? Leave him alone.

SOLDIER: What's your problem? Huh? The way you're looking at me pisses me off. That's supposed to be nothing, huh?

TEACHER: He's looking because he has eyes. If you have eyes, you look.

SOLDIER: But not in a way that's gonna piss me off. There aren't many who look that way. And I beat the shit out of them. Why get stewed otherwise? Right?

PHOEBE: IF YOU HAVE EYES, YOU LOOK.

BUTCHER: Prison is a test. You will mature as time goes by, and it'll seem to pass quickly.

GIRL: It's not going to get any less. It's something huge—like eternity. Is it eternity?

BUTCHER: That'd be bleak. Just think, someone'll be there to wake you up tomorrow morning. You'll have a cellmate. Night and day. Even when you're asleep he'll be there.

GIRL: But you have to *feel* something. Like you and your God. And I can't, and it makes me sick.

BUTCHER: The sickness is in your imagination. It doesn't attack your limbs or paralyze your joints. You can use prayer to fight diseased thoughts. "In all humility I beg your indulgence, Dear Lord," for example, and "Oh Lord of the Eucharist, Nourisher of Souls," and "Out of my deep need I cry unto Thee."

GIRL: And I'm condemned to this misery. Your prayers will make the sentence even longer. The Rosary beads will burn through my fingers. Purgatory's flames . . .

BUTCHER: The pain will ease as you suffer through it. It will consume itself and acquire meaning.

GIRL: Oh stars above, and love; oh pine the time! And blossoms, pain and heaven's eternal flame.

BUTCHER: It is not hunger; it is not thirst; it is not hate; it is not love. None of these things do you suffer—you only suffer suffering.

GIRL: Set me free!

PHOEBE: YOU WILL MATURE AS TIME GOES BY, AND IT'LL SEEM TO PASS QUICKLY. YOU CAN USE PRAYER TO FIGHT DISEASED THOUGHTS. YOU ONLY SUFFER SUFFERING.

MODEL: Of course you know Frau Hansen who used to live on the fourth floor.

THE MISTRESS: The redhead, the one with the arthritic husband?

MODEL: That's her. Get this, she divorced her husband.

THE MISTRESS: No!

MODEL: Yup. And that's not all. Four weeks later she married a migrant, a Turk!

THE MISTRESS: A Turk? God almighty!

MODEL: Yes. It wasn't enough to leave her sick husband out in the cold, but she goes and marries a foreigner.

THE MISTRESS: These days plenty have it hot for foreigners.

MODEL: Yeah. It takes all kinds. But I'd be so embarrassed, just embarrassed to be seen on the street with that sort.

THE MISTRESS: Right. But some people don't know what shame is.

PHOEBE: IT TAKES ALL KINDS. SOME PEOPLE DON'T KNOW WHAT SHAME IS.

SOLDIER: I was left-half.

BUTCHER: Yeah? I was goalie.

SOLDIER: Couldn't tell from the way you look now.

BUTCHER: What do you mean?

SOLDIER: I just mean. Got a little fat, didn't you?

BUTCHER: So? Better fat than poor.

SOLDIER: I don't know. It kills you quicker.

BUTCHER: Who cares? As long as I'm in this world I plan to have it good. After that doesn't interest me.

SOLDIER: I wouldn't want to be as fat as you.

BUTCHER: Envy, pure and simple. How much you make a week?

SOLDIER: Three hundred.

BUTCHER: Just three hundred. I'd rather be dead and buried.

SOLDIER: Oh yeah? How much you make?

BUTCHER: More'n you. That's for sure. I wouldn't do your job for that kind of cash.

SOLDIER: Oh yeah? There's a case of the wish being father to the thought.

PHOEBE: BETTER FAT THAN POOR. THERE'S A CASE OF THE WISH BEING FATHER TO THE THOUGHT.

POLICEMAN: Open your trap, slut. Name.

DEAD SOLDIER'S WIFE: Magda Schneider.

POLICEMAN: Born?

DEAD SOLDIER'S WIFE: April 12, 1935.

POLICEMAN: Marital status?

DEAD SOLDIER'S WIFE: Single.

POLICEMAN: What? At your age still single? I'd be ashamed of myself if I was you.

DEAD SOLDIER'S WIFE: Yeah. I never could find anyone who was right for me, or me for them.

POLICEMAN: Sad. But it doesn't surprise me. You don't even wash. Address.

DEAD SOLDIER'S WIFE: I lost my room. Couldn't pay. I was sick.

POLICEMAN: No permanent residence. Tsk, tsk. That's bad. You'll have to stay here.

PHOEBE: I'D BE ASHAMED OF MYSELF IF I WAS YOU. I WAS SICK.

SOLDIER: I was supposed to come. You sent for me.

LOVER: Your name?

SOLDIER: Kretschmar.

LOVER: Oh yes. That's right. It grieves me to have to tell you this, but as a consequence of our modernization the company has decided to let you go. You have notice as of the first.

SOLDIER: The company? . . . I've been on the job 26 years . . .

LOVER: The company considered many things. The company reached a decision. We can't tamper with decisions by the upper administration. What comes from above is final. That's how it is.

SOLDIER: It was the boss. I know. It's been happening a lot. Very modern.

LOVER: Just between us, are you in the union?

SOLDIER: No. Not my thing.

LOVER: Yeah, well, then.

PHOEBE: WHAT COMES FROM ABOVE IS FINAL. THAT'S HOW IT IS.

TEACHER: The system is very simple. You pay us ten thousand marks and we use it to build a car-wash. The money you collect from cars goes to pay off the ten thousand, and what's left is profit. You make money while you sleep. Such a deal.

BUTCHER: I have the money. There I'm ok. But I had to save a long time for it. You get attached to your savings.

TEACHER: Once you do these figures, the contract will practically sign itself. Look, we've worked out how you make your profit. If as few as three hundred cars a day go through the wash, in eight months you'll have your money back. The following nine years, four months is profits. You'll be able to put the money to good use elsewhere. After ten years, the carwash belongs to my company.

BUTCHER: And if I don't get three hundred cars a day?

TEACHER: Hey, look at the streets. What do you see? Cars! Come on!

PHOEBE: YOU GET ATTACHED TO YOUR SAVINGS.

DEAD SOLDIER'S WIFE: Act like he didn't even exist.

GIRL: But I can't. I blush just thinking about him.

DEAD SOLDIER'S WIFE: Not good. Not good at all. When they see you're an easy mark they pick you up and they dump you in the same motion.

GIRL: But why? I love him.

DEAD SOLDIER'S WIFE: Because a conquest makes a man feel good about himself. Otherwise he just has his fun and doesn't want to bother with the rest. That's how things are.

GIRL: I can't imagine anything dishonest like that about someone I love. That would be rotten.

DEAD SOLDIER'S WIFE: Then be stupid. Mark my words. There are human laws you have to respect if you want to be happy in this world.

PHOEBE: A CONQUEST MAKES A MAN FEEL GOOD ABOUT HIM-SELF. MARK MY WORDS.

THE MISTRESS: I can't love you.

BUTCHER: Don't say that. You're here with me now, and I won't let you go.

THE MISTRESS: Stop talking. Please stop talking. People can't always do what they want. Unless I'm there with him, he'll kill himself.

BUTCHER: Then he's insignificant, a cipher. He can't just suck your life away for the sake of his. That's not right.

THE MISTRESS: I loved that man, truly. We promised each other so much. People *have to* keep their promises.

BUTCHER: Not when it's over. You don't love him anymore, Renate, you don't love him anymore. Life under those conditions would be pure hell.

THE MISTRESS: I am involved—deeply. I can't just chuck that out. I love you, but there's no way.

PHOEBE: PEOPLE CAN'T ALWAYS DO WHAT THEY WANT. THEY HAVE TO KEEP THEIR PROMISES. LIFE UNDER THOSE CONDI-TIONS WOULD BE PURE HELL.

POLICEMAN: I put up the capital. Correct?

SOLDIER: You'll get it back.

POLICEMAN: But I've been working for ten years too. Hard.

SOLDIER: You got paid. I . . .

POLICEMAN: Listen, that investment has grown. My capital and my work pro-duced what we have today.

SOLDIER: Yeah.

POLICEMAN: Well, then half the money should actually belong to me.

SOLDIER: Could be. But the contracts say something else. And—I honor my contracts.

POLICEMAN: You're talking fraud. Because I made a stupid mistake once. You're taking advantage.

SOLDIER: Shut up! A contract's a contract! If you don't know that you'll have to learn it.

PHOEBE: I HONOR MY CONTRACTS.

LOVER: My . . .? Oh, of course. I remember.

BUTCHER: I don't mind running a tab, but that's a nice piece of change we're talking here.

LOVER: A . . . ? How much then?

BUTCHER: Yeah. Twelve hundred marks.

LOVER: Twelve hundred marks!!! Twelve hundred marks?

BUTCHER: Ask your wife. She ought to know. Am I supposed to know what goes on between you? Give me a break.

LOVER: Twelve hundred marks. That's crazy!

BUTCHER: Seeing how the amount upsets you this much I'm going to have to insist on exceptionally prompt repayment. Like right now. Maybe you just don't *have* the money, in which case I'm left standing here like a jerk. Sure is easy to misjudge character sometimes.

PHOBE: AM I SUPPOSED TO KNOW WHAT GOES ON BETWEEN YOU? GIVE ME A BREAK. SURE IS EASY TO MISJUDGE CHARACTER SOMETIMES.

SOLDIER: I'm going now.

GIRL: I know. Can you . . .

SOLDIER: No. No. There's no way. They hound you to the point of despair. You never stop.

GIRL: Yeah.

SOLDIER: Yeah. It was great being with you. When I die, then . . .

GIRL: Not that! You have to come back. I need you so much. You *can't* die.

SOLDIER: You can't choose how it's going to end. It happens, then you're fucked. Or maybe not—you come back and you can't shake the fear.

GIRL: They never gave us a chance. We're just fuel for their machine.

SOLDIER: Yeah. I'm going. I'm going now.

GIRL: Yeah. I love him so much.

PHOEBE: THEY HOUND YOU TO THE POINT OF DESPAIR. YOU NEVER STOP. I NEED YOU SO MUCH.

BUTCHER: I make sure the money angle runs smooth. That's real. Nothing else is.

POLICEMAN: Right.

BUTCHER: And then they're always going on about strikes and like that. They're just lazy bastards who don't want to do nothing.

POLICEMAN: Yeah. I don't know . . .

BUTCHER: Are you going to give me the same shit? I always figure everybody but me must be out of his mind.

POLICEMAN: I always did agree with what you say, but . . .

BUTCHER: Not for me, man, not for me. You got work, and you got money. I could do without the work part. Who couldn't? But the money, that I need. And no work, no money, unless you have some capital. I'm fucked. So I'm gonna hang in there, me and my lonesome. Why not? It's ok by me. None of that other shit for me.

POLICEMAN: Yeah, you're probably right. I don't want any aggravation either. I can see what you mean.

PHOEBE: NO WORK NO MONEY, UNLESS YOU HAVE SOME CAPITAL. I DON'T WANT ANY AGGRAVATION.

TEACHER: You must of course try to put all your observations to good use.

LOVER: Certainly. You can count on that.

THE MISTRESS: Good God almighty! Never!

BUTCHER: Don't misunderstand me. I'm just passing on what I've heard.

LOVER: Nonsense. You should know me better than that.

PHOEBE: YOUR MOTHER IS A BITCH.

THE MISTRESS: Pardon me? Did you hear that?

MODEL: Leave her alone. The poor thing.

THE MISTRESS: But there are limits.

SOLDIER: As for me, there's a lot I don't understand anymore. I try, but . . .

MODEL: What don't you understand anymore?

SOLDIER: That the situation, unless . . .

PHOEBE: THIEF TODAY, TOMORROW A KILLER.

TEACHER: Yes, popular wisdom. I wouldn't mock.

MODEL: (To Phoebe.) Come.

TEACHER: Who is that?

SOLDIER: Seems new here.

POLICEMAN: Darling. I'm glad to see you. Have you been here long?

MODEL: No, no. It's just as horrible as ever.

LOVER: Do you like the party?

PHOEBE: WHAT SHOULD I CARE ABOUT YOUR DOMESTIC PROBLEMS?

LOVER: Do we know each other?

GIRL: Astrology of course. What else is there to get involved in, huh?

DEAD SOLDIER'S WIFE: Yes.

PHOEBE: FOR ME, JUSTICE IS WHAT MATTERS.

GIRL: Darling. (Kisses her.) You're new, poor thing. Still confused.

PHOEBE: YOU GET USED TO EVERYTHING.

LOVER: She's a charming young lady.

GIRL: Yes.

THE MISTRESS: Master?!

TEACHER: Yes?

THE MISTRESS: Would you fetch me something to drink? Scotch please . . .

TEACHER: Gladly.

PHOEBE: I DON'T WANT TO GET INVOLVED IN TOO MUCH.

DEAD SOLDIER'S WIFE: A wise decision, darling, really. People spread themselves too thin.

GIRL: How was America?

LOVER: Fantastic. Really fantastic. The distances—incomparable.

GIRL: You lucky dog.

DEAD SOLDIER'S WIFE: Let's sit down.
PHOEBE: I'M AFRAID.
DEAD SOLDIER'S WIFE: A lot of people feel that way, darling. It's the contemporary disease.
THE MISTRESS: Thank you. And don't forget the book. You *did* promise.
TEACHER: Come on, you should know me better than that.
PHOEBE: THAT'S HOW IT IS.
BUTCHER: What?
LOVER: Pardon me. Would you like to dance?
PHOEBE: PEOPLE CHANGE THEIR MINDS.
BUTCHER: She's peculiar.
SOLDIER: More fun than talking business with you.
BUTCHER: Look, that has its place too.
POLICEMAN: And school?
MODEL: I'll bank on my looks.
POLICEMAN: Makes sense.
LOVER: Lovely, the way you dance.
PHOEBE: I'M FATIGUED.
LOVER: Already? Let's sit down.
DEAD SOLDIER'S WIFE: Italy. That's excitement!
THE MISTRESS: We're too quick to compromise ourselves.
PHOEBE: THAT'S TRUE. IT'S OK THAT THERE ARE DIFFERENCES IN THIS WORLD.
LOVER: You are beautiful.
PHOEBE: WHEN YOU'RE UNHAPPY, YOU HAVE TO TALK ABOUT IT.
SOLDIER: Pardon me. May I have a word with you?
LOVER: Sure. Just a second.
PHOEBE: I HAVE A PREMONITION OF THE END.
LOVER: I'll be right back. Really. (*To the Soldier.*) Yeah?
PHOEBE: I HAVE TO CONFRONT MY THOUGHTS.
SOLDIER: Do you know this person?
LOVER: No, but . . .
SOLDIER: She's behaving strangely.
LOVER: I don't know, I . . .
BUTCHER: I'm still looking for the truth.
GIRL: There's no such thing as an ultimate truth.
BUTCHER: We'll see.
DEAD SOLDIER'S WIFE: He forgot about you? Just like him. Uh huh.
PHOEBE: I DON'T WANT TO DIE.
DEAD SOLDIER'S WIFE: Please, darling. Are you a pessimist or something?
PHOEBE: WE'RE ALL AFRAID.
DEAD SOLDIER'S WIFE: Right again.
PHOEBE: THERE'S STILL SOMETHING BETWEEN US.

DEAD SOLDIER'S WIFE: The two of us. You are sweet. Really.

PHOEBE: WHO CARES?

DEAD SOLDIER'S WIFE: I get the feeling you're drunk.

MODEL: I have to mingle a little.

POLICEMAN: Of course, I'm sorry.

MODEL: I'll be back. In a minute. What does that awful creature want from you? He's always getting so worked up.

LOVER: It's the girl. Thinks there's something weird about her.

MODEL: Just between us, she *is* a little peculiar. Good luck anyway.

LOVER: Thanks. Sorry, it took longer than I thought.

PHOEBE: I NEED YOU.

LOVER: I don't know . . . I guess I could like you too. Really.

MODEL: Having fun?

TEACHER: Tolerable. Thanks.

MODEL: Yes. We're expecting more people, then it's sure to pick up.

THE MISTRESS: Darling, wasn't that actor supposed to come tonight?

LOVER: Heavens no. What are you thinking? I respect him as an artist, that's all.

PHOEBE: YOU MAKE ME WANT TO PUKE.

LOVER: I . . . the . . . Why so suddenly?

PHOBE: PAMPERING LEAVES ITS MARK.

DEAD SOLDIER'S WIFE: He's certainly fast.

GIRL: He's always fast. That's his specialty.

PHOEBE: A STRICT UPBRINGING IS THE BEST INTRODUCTION TO LIFE.

LOVER: You've had too much to drink. Please, we're attracting attention.

PHOBE: MY FEET HURT.

LOVER: Let's go.

PHOEBE: PACK YOUR THINGS.

LOVER: Come on. I don't understand.

PHOEBE: YOU DON'T HAVE TO WORK. YOU JUST RAKE IN THE GOODIES.

LOVER: Behave yourself, I . . .

PHOEBE: NO ONE TAKES NOTHING AWAY FROM ME.

LOVER: Come on honey, you'll be ok.

PHOEBE: I LOVE YOU. (*She bites the Lover.*)

LOVER: Despair I accept, of course.

TEACHER: We all do. No question.

PHOEBE: WE ALL HURT EACH OTHER.

LOVER: These are Nature's laws. We learn. Scotch.

TEACHER: Thanks. A discussion to finish up with. Indeed.

PHOEBE: YOU ARE BEAUTIFUL.

THE MISTRESS: (*Cold.*) Hah! It's rare for one woman to compliment another.

TEACHER: Ever rarer when she means it. Come on.

THE MISTRESS: Thank you. Here's to you.

PHOEBE: IT DEPRESSES ME.

THE MISTRESS: What does, darling?

PHOEBE: PAIN IS THE PRICE YOU PAY.

GIRL: Now that is a banal observation. But come to think of it not without value.

THE MISTRESS: And are you any deeper in love? I'm still having trouble.

PHOEBE: BEAUTIFUL THINGS NEVER LAST LONG.

THE MISTRESS: Isn't that the case?

DEAD SOLDIER'S WIFE: But you have such a charming husband. Come now.

THE MISTRESS: All that glitters is not gold.

PHOEBE: KISS ME.

THE MISTRESS: Who? Me?

MODEL: I almost think she means you.

SOLDIER: And now the pit gapes wide. Do you know the story of Pelleas and Melisande?

BUTCHER: No. And I'm not interested either.

SOLDIER: You really are a philistine.

PHOEBE: I DON'T WANT TO LIVE WITH ANOTHER HUMAN BEING.

GIRL: Oh, everyone does. If you're alone . . .

MODEL: Where there's a will there's a way.

PHOEBE: THAT SOUNDS ROTTEN.

LOVED ONE: You oughtn't hurt your friends.

PHOEBE: I HAVE TO BE CAREFUL.

POLICEMAN: You're all shitheads.

MODEL: Franz! Please!

LOVED ONE: Don't worry. We all know his condition.

PHOEBE: NATURE'S LAWS. (*She bites the Mistress.*)

POLICEMAN: I hate all of you!

MODEL: Don't drink anymore Franz. Listen.

PHOEBE: YOU'RE GOING TO DIE.

SOLDIER: Does she mean me? She means me. She said I'm going to die.

MODEL: Calm down.

SOLDIER: Of course I'm going to die. You're all going to die.

PHOBE: LIAR.

DEAD SOLDIER'S WIFE: You know, this kind of party follows its own rules.

PHOBE: YOU WILL FEEL PITY FOR YOURSELF.

POLICEMAN: Pity? What's that?

SOLDIER: I said it right away. She's cracked.

GIRL: I don't know, I think she's nice.

PHOEBE: STOP IT!

GIRL: But I said I like you.

PHOEBE: YOU HAVE TO BE ABLE TO TAKE CARE OF YOURSELF.

MODEL: Darling. Let's sit down.

PHOEBE: ARE YOU TRYING TO START SOMETHING?

MODEL: No, no. I only wanted to have a nice little talk with you.

PHOEBE: YOU'RE JUST JEALOUS.

MODEL: Jealous?! What do you mean by that? You have to accept certain restraints, even if you are a stranger. Jealous! (*She cries.*)

PHOEBE: WHO STILL BELIEVES IN ETERNITY THESE DAYS?

BUTCHER: No one. Hardly anyone. I know all about that.

PHOEBE: I'M JUST HONEST. (*She bites the Model.*)

TEACHER: Maybe she's right. Maybe it's a kind of honesty that's new to us.

PHOEBE: YOU MAY LICK MY FEET.

TEACHER: My dear friend, you can't start a fight with me that easily.

PHOEBE: GET OFF YOU MANGY SHIT. YOU ALWAYS TREAT ME SO BADLY.

TEACHER: But I just met the lady.

PHOEBE: WHEN SOMEONE MAKES FUN OF ME, I GO NUTS. YOU UNDERSTAND?

DEAD SOLDIER'S WIFE: A rather vulgar person.

GIRL: Do you know why she was invited?

DEAD SOLDIER'S WIFE: No idea. I find it all quite tasteless.

BUTCHER: Perhaps you'd like to talk business after all.

SOLDIER: Yeah now.

PHOEBE: I'M EMBARRASSED. WE DIDN'T WANT TO CRAMP EACH OTHER.

POLICEMAN: Pack of stinking little bastards.

DEAD SOLDIER'S WIFE: That one's behaving just impossibly too.

PHOEBE: I NEED TO BE FREE. I MIGHT HAVE BEEN ABLE TO BEAR IT. YOU ALWAYS WANTED TO USE ME.

DEAD SOLDIER'S WIFE: I'm sure you're confusing me with someone, darling.

PHOEBE: THE CHILD NEVER LOVED ME.

DEAD SOLDIER'S WIFE: Still she's unusual.

POLICEMAN: The lady's a good looker. Where you from?

PHOEBE: I LOVE BEING WITH YOU SO MUCH.

POLICEMAN: With me? Yeah, I can see that.

PHOEBE: NO ONE CAN STAND IT ALONE FOR VERY LONG. DON'T TOUCH ME. OUR FATHER WHO ART IN HEAVEN, FORGIVE ME. I THINK YOU'RE BEAUTIFUL.

POLICEMAN: Hey this lady's wild. Real wild. I think you're terrific, honey. Something else.

DEAD SOLDIER'S WIFE: See? Birds of a feather flock together.

GIRL: That's how it is. Some things you can be sure of.

PHOEBE: I ADORE YOU. I'D LIKE TO SLEEP WITH YOU.

POLICEMAN: Where'd you come from? Tell us.

PHOEBE: WITHOUT TRUST NOTHING'S POSSIBLE. A CHILD IS YOURS, REALLY YOURS.

POLICEMAN: She has an imagination. You assholes. This lady has ideas in her head, not like you bunch of wet rags.

DEAD SOLDIER'S WIFE: Aren't we being brash!

PHOEBE: IF YOU HAVE EYES, YOU LOOK.

BUTCHER: Want to leave? We could have a drink somewhere else.

DEAD SOLIDER'S WIFE: Darling?

GIRL: Hell no, it's just getting exciting.

DEAD SOLDIER'S WIFE: Then we'll stay a while longer.

PHOEBE: YOU'LL MATURE AS TIME GOES BY AND IT'LL SEEM TO PASS QUICKLY. YOU CAN USE PRAYER TO FIGHT DISEASED THOUGHTS. YOU'LL MATURE AS TIME GOES BY AND IT'LL SEEM TO PASS QUICKLY.

POLICEMAN: I love you. I love this woman, and I hate the rest of you.

SOLDIER: You're behaving badly. Think of what you're saying.

POLICEMAN: You little shit.

SOLDIER: OK, pal, OK.

PHOEBE: YOU ONLY SUFFER SUFFERING. (*She bites the Dead Soldier's Wife.*) IT TAKES ALL KINDS.

POLICEMAN: Come back here. Come on.

PHOEBE: SOME PEOPLE DON'T KNOW WHAT SHAME IS.

TEACHER: You, of all people.

PHOEBE: BETTER FAT THAN POOR.

TEACHER: You calling me fat? Huh?

PHOEBE: A CASE OF THE WISH BEING FATHER TO THE THOUGHT. I'D BE ASHAMED OF MYSELF IF I WAS YOU.

TEACHER: You *are* crazy, you know that.

GIRL: That's what I said right off the bat. And I'm not wrong very often.

POLICEMAN: I've been dropped. I'm alone.

PHOEBE: WHAT COMES FROM ABOVE, IS FINAL. THAT'S HOW IT IS.

BUTCHER: What now? You like the business or not?

PHOEBE: YOU GET ATTACHED TO YOUR SAVINGS.

BUTCHER: You can do what you like. Be my guest. But you better leave my business to me.

PHOEBE: A CONQUEST MAKES A MAN FEEL GOOD ABOUT HIMSELF. MARK MY WORDS.

GIRL: Sometimes I think she hits the nail right on the head.

TEACHER: She's plastered. You can tell.

GIRL: You're probably right.

PHOEBE: PEOPLE CAN'T ALWAYS DO WHAT THEY WANT.

GIRL: Right. That's something you in particular shouldn't forget.

POLICEMAN: I have to . . . something to . . . something to drink, because I . . . some more . . .

PHOEBE: THEY HAVE TO KEEP THEIR PROMISES. LIFE UNDER THOSE CONDITIONS WOULD BE PURE HELL. (*She bites the Girl.*)

TEACHER: When I think of it the whole evening is kind of funny.

BUTCHER: I don't know. There's no point to it.

POLICEMAN: Human beings are rotten. All of them.

BUTCHER: I can never figure how people can let themselves get so drunk. No self control.

TEACHER: Mostly it's just unhappy people who drink like that. They don't know how to get on.

PHOEBE: I HONOR MY CONTRACTS.

POLICEMAN: You shut up. You're as bad as the rest of them.

PHOEBE: AM I SUPPOSED TO KNOW WHAT GOES ON BETWEEN YOU? (*She bites the Policeman.*)

BUTCHER: They're all drunk. No sense of decorum.

TEACHER: You're right. So much is allowed to slip.

SOLDIER: There's something comical about life.

TEACHER: Now he's starting too. Come on!

BUTCHER: Are you feeling sick?

SOLDIER: No, I'm using my brain.

PHOEBE: GIVE ME A BREAK. (*She bites the Teacher.*)

BUTCHER: Don't you think we should leave? The party's winding down.

SOLDIER: I'm staying, understand?

BUTCHER: I just want what's best.

SOLDIER: Leave him alone.

PHOEBE: SURE IS EASY TO MISJUDGE CHARACTER SOMETIMES.

BUTCHER: Can't you shut your mouth? All this confusion is your fault.

PHOEBE: THEY HOUND YOU TO THE POINT OF DESPAIR.

SOLDIER: There's something to what she says.

BUTCHER: Come off it, you're all drunk.

SOLDIER: I'm not drunk.

BUTCHER: Every drunk claims he's sober as a judge. Every one.

PHOEBE: YOU NEVER STOP. (*She bites the Butcher.*)

SOLDIER: It's so quiet.

PHOEBE: I NEED YOU SO MUCH.

SOLDIER: I've never been any use to anyone. Not yet.

PHOEBE: NO WORK, NO MONEY.

SOLDIER: That's right. No work, no money.

PHOEBE: UNLESS YOU HAVE SOME CAPITAL.

SOLDIER: But I don't have any capital. You coming home with me, honey?

PHOEBE: I DON'T WANT ANY AGGRAVATION. (*She bites the Soldier.*)

LOVER: I don't know . . . once I . . . once I knew how . . .

MODEL: I can no longer . . . I forgot . . . I forgot the word.

TEACHER: But you can . . . I don't understand . . .

LOVER: Walk . . . the word is walk . . .

SOLDIER: I forgot . . . how . . .

DEAD SOLDIER'S WIFE: The words . . .

GIRL: Move-ment.

BUTCHER: Move—that was . . .

POLICEMAN: Forgot. I forgot.

THE MISTRESS: The one . . .

BUTCHER: How do you walk? How . . .

DEAD SOLDIER'S WIFE: How . . . is . . .

TEACHER: How can . . . how can you . . .

GIRL: What's my name?

LOVED ONE: What's . . .

SOLDIER: For-got.

PHOEBE: IT IS THROUGH THE CONCEPTUAL FACULTY THAT UNDERSTANDING USUALLY FINDS EXPRESSION; AND THUS IS IT DIFFERENTIATED FROM THE FACULTY OF JUDGMENT, AND DEDUCTION AS THE FACULTY OF FORMAL REASON. IT IS FOR THE MOST PART, HOWEVER, SET IN OPPOSITION TO REASON; BUT BY UNDERSTANDING IS NOT MEANT THE COMPREHENSION OF A GROUP OF CONCEPTS ALTOGETHER, RATHER OF CERTAIN SPECIFIC CONCEPTS, INDICATING THAT A CONCEPT MUST BE SPECIFIC IN ORDER TO EXIST AT ALL. IF UNDERSTANDING IN THIS SENSE IS DIFFERENTIATED FROM THE FACULTIES OF FORMAL JUDGMENT AND FORMAL REASON, THEN IT IS TO BE TAKEN AS THE ABILITY TO COMPREHEND INDIVIDUAL SPECIFIC CONCEPTS. FOR JUDGMENT AND DEDUCTION, OR REASON, ARE, IN THEIR FORMAL SENSE, ONLY ASPECTS OF WHAT IS UNDERSTOOD, IN THAT THEY APPEAR AS FORMS OF ABSTRACT CONCEPTUAL ANALYSIS. A CONCEPT IS NOT, HOWEVER, DETERMINED IN A PURELY ABSTRACT MANNER; UNDERSTANDING IS TO BE DIFFERENTIATED FROM REASON, THEREFORE, IN THE COMPREHENSION OF CONCEPTS AS A WHOLE.

END

# *Pre-Paradise Sorry Now*

Four basic sets of material make up the play:
 15 contres: scenes about the fascistoid underpinnings of everyday life, in which pairs
 gang up on individuals.
 6 narrations about the murderers Ian Brady and Myra Hindley.
 9 pas des deux: fictitious dialogues between the murderers.
 9 liturgical sections: texts reminiscent of the cannibalism embedded in liturgies and
 cults.

One can arrange the parts of the play however one sees fit, as long as the through-line
can be followed. In any case, the Ian/Myra dialogues should hold the dramaturgic
center. This published version conforms to the Stuttgart production (Director: Peer
Raben.) The pattern for the Munich premiere is attached in an appendix.

Optimal cast: 30 performers.
Minimal cast: 5 performers.

IAN BRADY I

It was at that time the business with the cat occurred. Ian had begun collecting Nazi memorabilia and regularly broke into a crumbling house near a bombed-out cemetery in the city center. There one day in the house—its outer structure was still intact—he ran across a cat. Up 'til then he had never had anything against cats. He wasn't particularly fond of them either. But now he had something against them. He caught the animal, stuffed it into a Ma Sloan's shopping bag, waited until dark and then shut the yowling animal up into an empty grave whose cover stone he had earlier jarred loose. The next day on the cricket field he asked his schoolmate Angus Morristown: "I bet you don't know how long a buried cat can stay alive?" Then he told the story. Angus didn't believe Ian so he went to the cemetery with a friend, opened the grave, and the cat jumped out. Ian had proved to his friends that he was "tough." He proved it again with the de-panting episode. A few of the boys had grabbed bashful Billie and de-panted him to have a good laugh at his skinny little manhood. They all yelled, "Ladyfinger." Ian stood there and smoked, until they wanted to de-pant him too.

H + K – I

K: Ya had someone in again last night.
I: That's my business.
K: It ain't just your business. Accordin' to the law.
H: If it happens again, you get notice.
K: Yeah, that's how it is, cuz we ain't interested in being liable. Get that

through your thick skull.

I: Who's going to pay you a hundred and fifty for a room like this where you can't even have a little privacy.

H: You watch your smart mouth! I called your company to see if you were still working there. What do you think they told me?

I: What?

H: That you ain't been on the job for three weeks.

K: So how do you make your living now? Or don't you want us to know?

I: Do I ask you how well you're shitting in the toilet?

H: Ok that's it! On the first you're out. You got your notice, definite.

K: After the first we don't want to see you.

I: Yeah sure, but I get my deposit back at least.

H: Don't talk crap. We're covered in ways you can only dream about. That is, if you're not too far gone even to dream about it.

K: I don't even wanna know what's gonna become of her.

I+L−M

I: Why did you spread that stuff around about us?

L: You think it's right they're all talking about us?

M: That's just how people talk.

L: No, not "just how people talk." —I hold you responsible. I could kick your ass for this.

I: Sounds good to me. Kick away.

L: Real good.

I: Do it, go ahead.

L: Maybe. What about you? Got a better idea?

M: What do you mean?

L: Something. You better believe it.

M: I don't understand a word of what you're saying.

L: Then think it over. Just consider it a second. No idea? Nothing? How about now?

M: Just tell me for chrissake. What do you mean?

L: I'm thinking of a little settlement. Geetus. Ca-ash.

I: Brilliant. You're brilliant.

M: I don't have any money. Not much anyhow.

L: But that little you have. You will of course turn that over voluntarily. To make up for the personal damages you've caused.

I: Move, pal. The wallet.

M: Ok. Twenty bucks.

L: Twenty bucks?

M: Yeah. Or what?

I: Now *you* can give him a little encouragement.

## L+M−K

M: You're my friend. I've already been in India, Nepal, almost got to China.
L: What about Norway, Finland? The North is great. Finnish women.
M: I dig the South.
L: Hey look at that one. Some belly! And a carnation in his buttonhole.
M: Shoe leather—two hundred yards, max! Then it's strictly BMWs and the elevator scene.
K: I eat whatever I feel like. Because I work. Telephoning makes you hungry. Fresh air can give you an appetite too.
M: Check out your cheeks. Son of Hamster!
K: Like I said I work for my cheeks.
M: Hamsters'd dig you, pal.
K: Because I'm on my own, nowhere to hang out. If I had someplace, the picture'd be different. Completely different.
L: This kick in your shins makes me happy.
M: What makes me happy is beating on your head.
L: And this uppercut to your chin.
M: And this left hook to your spleen.
L: Breaking bones.
M: The kind with bellies attached.
K: Let me buy you a beer.
M: Now that sounds better. In fact much better.
L: Let's go. Beer city!

***

IAN: I'm coming to your party tonight.
MYRA: Yes.
IAN: I will bring wine.
MYRA: You don't have to, we . . .
IAN: German wine.
MYRA: Of course. I'll tell mother and father about you. I haven't mentioned you yet.
IAN: That's alright. I will be there at eight. On the dot. You can count on me.
MYRA: I'm sure of that.
IAN: With certainty. Not that I want to discuss *myself*.
MYRA: I guess I can appreciate that about you.
IAN: You appear to be quite clever. Just looking at you I can tell.
MYRA: Thank you. I'm not fishing for compliments.
IAN: Nevertheless I would like to point out that your hair color meets with my approval.
MYRA: I thought I'd know your taste.
IAN: Your judgment is sound.
MYRA: There will be something to eat too.

IAN: I eat very little  Do sports. Hike in the woods. To me, physical condition-
ing is second only to mental concentration.

MYRA: I will want to join you.

IAN: It will tone your muscles.

MYRA: I won't forget that.

IAN: The era of the strong will arrive. Those who listen to me will be at the
forefront of that era.

MYRA: I will listen to you.

IAN: We must never forget the hour of our grief.

***

C: Despise this world, lest ye perish with it.

EVERYONE: The heavens proclaim the glory of God and the firmament the
work of thy hand.

C: Despise this world, lest . . .

EVERYONE: Thou coverest the heavens with clouds and showest the winds their
path.

C: Despise this world . . .

EVERYONE: Thou causest the fields to prosper and comfortest us with food and
drink.

C: Despise this world . . .

***

IAN: I showed you the photographs. What effect did they have on you?

MYRA: They turned me on. I was ready to get hot. They're powerful, my
Führer.

IAN: Can you imagine a time when what we have going won't be enough?

MYRA: If you wish it.

IAN: The front we put up when we're not here. This "just friends" business. It's
oppressive. Being polite to everyone. It's not easy for me. And then again it
is.

MYRA: I feel as you do.

IAN: You stand above the multitude, Hessie. I appreciate your value as my deputy. Your eyes gleam with the dignity of pride.

MYRA: I am glad to satisfy your expectations.

IAN: Be German. That is your goal.

MYRA: You make me worthy, my Führer.

IAN: Fetch some wine, Hessie. Liebfraumilch.

MYRA: I don't have any more money. Can you help out? Please?

IAN: Are you crazy? You spent it all! This imprudence of yours will have to be
punished.

MYRA: I thank you, my Führer. Your indulgence is great.

IAN: You shall have mercy.

MYRA: I thank you.

IAN: The mercy is mine.

L+M−H

L: Nice piece of cunt.
M: Horny piece of cunt.
L: Let's fuck her.
M: Gotta do it. Now.
H: No, please don't.
L: Heel, bitch. Don't we turn you on?
H: If you don't let me go, I'll scream. (*Screams.*)
M: Scream away, cunt. Nobody's gonna hear you.
H: Please, please. Let me go.
L: Oooh, makes us hot when you yell like that. Go ahead, yell.
H: Help! Help!
M: Ha. Yeah. Hold her arms tight.
L: Right.
H: Mommy! Mommy!
M: You can yell for mommy all you want.
L: I wish she *was* here. Then we'd have one apiece.
M: You dirty slut, don't scratch me. You *do* want it, don't you? Admit it. Ow! What are you, crazy?
L: Yeah, she's crazy.
H: No kissing. Please, no kissing.
L: Why not? Don't you like my mouth? I brushed them this morning. Just like you're supposed to.
M: Ok, no fooling now. Hold her arms. Still got your cherry, sister? I'm gonna carve it up with my little knife.
L: It's nice, honey. Believe me, real nice.

H+K−L

K: We gotta talk. Serious. About d'future.
H: Don't be too strick wit'm. He ain't all there.
L: You tellin' me I'm not all there.
H: Come on, just a little, you know. Slow, but he's ok.
K: It don' interest me. I wanna know about the money angle. The pocketbook, nothin' else.
L: What's he mean?
H: How much a week you make? Whatta ya got in the bank? That kinda thing.
L: Hundred eighty a week. Gross. Nine hundred twenty in the bank. Franklin Savings and Loan.
K: You gonna keep a woman on that? You oughta be ashamed.
L: S'gonna get betta.
K: A wet fart maybe, but money that ain't. Blush! Go ahead! Cause you should

be embarrassed.

H: That ain't too much, I guess, yeah.

K: You serious all of a sudden? About him?

L: No kiddin'. S'gonna get betta.

K: Betta, worse. That kinda money it don' make no difference.

H: But the physical thing—you know—that's pretty good.

K: Then stick to the physical, and drop them other ideas.

H + L – I

L: Now that is one beautiful girl.

I: That one?

L: Yeah. Yeah. You know her?

I: Sure. Come over here you.

H: You want something from me?

L: How much you get?

H: What's it worth to you?

L: Well . . . I don't know.

H: You have to say.

L: Fifty?

H: Ok.

I: But you picked me.

L: Yeah, before.

I: That's not right.

L: Look, I'll pay you anyway. Ok?

I: Yeah, sure.

L: God, you are beautiful.

H: Oh?

L: Yeah, and you know it.

H: Maybe so.

L: You turn me on. You here a lot?

H: I work here.

L: But I've never seen you.

H: Yeah. I always go quick.

L: I guess so. Should we go?

H: Sure. The sooner the better.

L: Right. See you.

H: Bye now. Be happy, hear!

I: Yeah, but being happy ain't always fun.

## IAN BRADY II

All Ian said, real quiet like, was "Ok, ok." We were knocked out. He pressed the cigarette between his lips to free his hands. "Well, then," he said, "what can

I show you?" "Ok, gentlemen," he said, and then as if he were fetching something very valuable out of a bag—he took it out, cigarette in the corner of his mouth, face shrouded in smoke. And for a growing boy it was certainly a strapping thing, and it wasn't even hard yet. Well we had to give him credit. He was odds-on favorite. Then Ian left school, worked as a delivery boy, and then for a butcher. He read mysteries and occasionally on long winter evenings he'd break into houses. Ian was almost seventeen when the police caught him again. But he just got probation for the third time. Condition: that he stay with his natural mother, Maggie Stewart. And so it was that Ian moved out of the Glasgow slums into the much worse ones in Manchester. All he took with him were some newspaper clippings about Hitler and a well-worn paperback copy of *The Third Man.*

H+K−M

H: The boy made indecent advances toward me. It was blatant. Normally I don't get this way. You know me. I'm liberal with young people. Everyone knows that. But there are limits.
K: How did it happen?
H: It was shower-time. I suppose you know the new grouping puts the young ones in the shower together with the sixteen to eighteen year olds. Much as I regret to say it, young people don't really scrub themselves without supervision. And then, oh how horrible . . .
K: Stop crying, dear. What did you do to her to upset her like this?
H: He has to be punished. Punish him! The parents must be informed. Who knows? We may have a potential sex fiend here.
K: That's correct. In these matters we can't be careful enough. What can you say in your own defense? What did you do to her?
H: He's being stubborn. Incredible. I would like to stress how this ties in with his schoolwork. It's been sliding. What happened doesn't really surprise me.
K: How interesting. So your academic work leaves something to be desired too. The schoolboy lust is no big surprise then.
H: He reached under my sweater and grabbed my breast.
K: I thought it was something like that. The incident must be reported to his parents. People like to know what they're raising.
H: And spending their money on. And denying themselves for.
K: People like to know. And your parents are sure to be interested in this little episode.
H: I'm sure of that.

H+L−M

K: Who shit his pants and crammed them in the toilet? Mr. Pisser and Moaner! That's who. Clear as day.

L: The toilet's stuffed up. He jerked off last night too. Bedstains. I saw them.

K: Mister Pisser and Moaner! And pigged up the shithouse walls with all kinds of graffiti. And who messed up the table—the slob did the job, that's who.

M: [*English original.*] Hand in hand. Hand in it. It in it. That's it.

K: (*Contra publico.*) Did you jerk off last night?

L: I don't care about them. But he's different. I know all about him.

K: That sort of graffiti undermines the men's morale. A pocketknife! Do you have a pocketknife?

L: Yes.

K: On the ground. Opened. Ready for action.

L: Laying and ready. Ready to cut.

K: Corporal Markus!

M: Reporting!

K: You know the game! Push-ups over open weapon.

M: At your command, sir.

K: Men like us need kicks, and when we need them we get them. Men like us— we're on the way. We're gonna be all that we can be.

L: Seven. Eight. Nine. Ten.

H, I: (*To those doing push-ups.*) [*English original.*] I wanna be loved by you.

## K+L–H

K: But you were friends.

H: You know that already.

L: When did you last see him?

H: Last week, Wednesday or Thursday.

L: And where did you meet him?

H: In a café. I think it was the Capri.

K: This pistol! Is it yours?

H: Yes.

K: He was shot with this pistol.

H: I didn't do anything. It wasn't me. Leave me alone.

L: When was the last time you saw the pistol?

H: A month ago. Maybe two.

K: Didn't you notice it was lost?

H: Maybe.

L: And why didn't you report it?

H: It didn't seem that important.

K: Why did you murder him?

H: It wasn't me. Why would I want to murder him? It wasn't me.

L: Let's just say—jealousy.

H: I could never be jealous of him.

L: Talk! We asked you a question.

K: Out with it! Why didn't you report the lost weapon?
L: Why did you shoot him?
K: Where were you last night between two and three?
L: Didn't he promise to marry you?
K: Out with it! Talk! You're not dealing with children here.

*** 

(*A tape of Myra crying.*)

IAN: You know why I had to hit you.
MYRA: You always know what you are doing. And I too am beginning to realize.
IAN: You will never make a mistake twice, Hessie. You will not disobey an order.
MYRA: I am here to learn.
IAN: I bought a book. Reading it has taken me one step further. Hessie, I would like you to read me a passage from it.
MYRA: I will do my best.
IAN: Here. Begin on this page.
MYRA: Justine had the fat baldhead priest up her anus. He caused her tremendous pain, but if she cried out it would mean the death penalty. The priest stuck it in her with incredible force and she let out an involuntary whimper. Father Jacques then called out, "Come my brothers, chastise this wayward creature. Fetch the cat o'nine tails." The other priests came and brought all manner of torture instruments with them. Justine had all she could do to remain conscious. Father Jacques withdrew his gigantic member from her anus, and her body began to relax just as the first blow landed—precisely between her legs. Father Jacques said, "I need a woman as cold and inhuman as I am. One who will carry out without question my every command."

*** 

A:
  God's will is supreme
  And it shall be fulfilled.
B:
  Wash that which is tainted
  Heal that which is wounded
  Quench that which suffers thirst.
C:
  Thy will be done on earth as it is in heaven.
B:
  Bend that which is rigid
  Warm that which is frigid
  Guide that which has become lost.

A:
God's will is supreme
And it shall be fulfilled.

\*\*\*

IAN: You behaved as I've come to expect. You have learned.

MYRA: I almost become skeptical when that policeman—remember—when he came up to me.

IAN: Very good, Hessie. You have demonstrated your worthiness. We'll continue our experiments.

MYRA: I stand ready to perform as commanded.

IAN: Now that you have proven yourself, your suggestions will be considered. I expressly allow it. There must be an elite, even if it is small. Of that I am sure. A vanguard. You, Myra, are part of that vanguard.

MYRA: My Führer, nothing could make me any happier.

IAN: The boy should have been kept alive longer. When we continue our experiments the food deprivation phase must be extended. The important thing is energy-withdrawal among inferior life forms.

MYRA: The windows and doors must be sealed, noise leakage avoided.

IAN: Good, Hessie. Fetch wine. Then we'll think the rest through. No?

MYRA: As you speak it, so it is.

IAN: Submission is the correct path for the masses. To submit, fully conscious— that is their happiness, that and nothing else.

# H + I − K

H: How much so far today?

I: Fifty.

H: Not bad. What's *he* want? Are you nuts?

K: What do you mean? I have rights too.

H: This here ain't no place for faggots.

I: You want to mess up our business?

K: Don't bug me, you'll be better off.

H: Perverts screw up our image around here.

K: Come off it, honey. Once they see my ass, you're in for a bull market.

H: Asses are for grabbing, that's all.

K: Not mine.

I: Ok beat it. Or I call the boss.

K: Is he the hot and horny type?

I: What's it to you, shithead? He ain't nothing.

K: Come off it, sweetie. I just want to know if he has a dick, a wild and crazy dick. That's the kind I dream about. Every night.

H: Christ is this one sick!

I: Ever got it on with a woman?

K: Come off it, do I look like a lesbian? Hmmm? Not for me, thanks.
I: Fucking fags, makes you puke.
H: The fairy brotherhood.
I: Loving brothers.
H: Get the fuck out of here anyhow.

K+M−L

K: How was Little Rock? I mean the car race. How much did you make?
L: You know, not bad. It's a living.
M: Some job you pulled too, huh!!!
L: What job? What are you talking about?
K: We just want to know who was boss. The boss, get it? Hmmm? Talk!
L: Ow! I . . . hey, ow . . . I don't know the names. There were two of them.
M: Let him go.
L: There was a woman too.
M: Was it Myra?
K: See. Ok.
M: Where are they? Both of them.
L: They screwed me. Like all the rest.
K: Use your head. Go ahead.
M: How does the cigarette taste like this?
K: Tell us, darling. Then we'll be real nice.
M: Stubborn little bastard.
K: Be nice.
L: She owns a bar in Dallas. Now quit it!
M: Sweetheart Myra, a bar in Dallas. What do you know.
L: I didn't get anything. Nothing.
M: Let's get on with it.
K: Ok.
L: What are you going to do? No. No. (Boot.) Hey! You didn't have to do that. I
    wouldn't have told . . .
M: Poor rat. Tiny little rat.

H+I−M

H: I'm a charter member of SAFF. If that makes you drool it's your own fault.
I: S-A-F-F: Sexual Activity Fast and Frequent.
H: Fuckyourself, as they say in the USA. That's what I say to you.
I: God knows there are better looking men.
H: And better in bed.
I: Has he even got one?
H: Not very big, as far as I can tell.

I: Hair on his chest?

H: Not much. Sweet ass though. I'd be happy if he'd just lie on his belly. Real sweet ass. As for the rest . . .

M: Why are you turning on me? You said it was like God's angels singing in heaven. And the way you moaned, and sweat like a pig. You.

H: I know what the guys with little weenies want. They want to feel like Tarzan.

I: (*Laughs.*)

H: Basically I prefer foreign cock to the domestic variety. Some of them though —wink and they come. All over themselves.

I: Did you screw the one with the eagles on his chest?

H: Wow! Talk about a humping machine!

M: (*Groans, moans.*)

H: Oh, yeah. Moan away. On the high wire without a net. But the decisions— they've been made.

M: Think it over. I'll give you three days.

H: (*Laughter, clear as a bell.*)

## IAN BRADY III

First he worked as a bag boy and shop assistant. Then he was unemployed, went on welfare, and started to steal again. Then two years in reform school, one more in a half-way house. When he got out things improved. He took up bookkeeping, and one day got a job with Millwarts Limited, a medium-size producer of soaps and oils. He stayed there almost seven years and eventually was put in charge of the orders department. He was reserved and kept to himself—always quiet except for the occasional fit of rage. No one got close to him, or noticed him—until one day a new stenographer was hired: Myra Hindley. The girl, tall and haughty, had an invalid father and a mother who was a machinist. She went to school where her 109 IQ was a little above average. Since the other girls in the neighborhood already had boyfriends, Myra still hung around with little Michael Higgins from the next block. She treated him like a doll, spoiled him and protected him from the bigger boys. Then one summer afternoon the doll got smashed. Michael Higgins drowned while swimming and Myra Hindley drowned in grief.

## K + M − I

M: Fun? Walking the streets?

I: It's ok.

K: Real fucking pigs, whores. Man-crazy pigs.

I: No one's making you do it.

K: You bet your ass. Not me.

M: How much you get?

I: Thirty for a trick in a car. Hotel costs fifty.
M: So? You any good?
I: Front and back, in the mouth. Whatever your heart desires.
K: Kiss my ass.
M: He ain't all wrong. Considering you do it with everyone.
I: All sorts of cock—big, small, washed, unwashed.
M: Don't you whores spread disease?
I: Just the opposite. We get regular checks-ups, us.
K: So you think you're worth fifty?
I: Depends what you like.
K: I wouldn't waste two bucks on her. Not me.
I: On your wife you would. That's what she gets, right? And she's better, huh?
K: Shut up about my wife.
M: His wife. There's a respectable woman. Nothing doing with her.
I: I'm respectable too. In my way. And honest.
K: You honest? With your eyes, and that face?
I: In my heart's where I'm respectable.
K: Don't make me laugh.

I+K–H

H: Desire, wild and rapturous. The soul shudders. (*Epileptic fit. Continuous.*)
K: I sent for the ambulance.
H: Grey shadows in front of my lids. Lemons and hyacinths.
I: Cut the crap.
K: Let her alone. I can see her arms in the straight-jacket already, and it makes
    me squirm. But out of pure lust.
I: You!
K: Right. Now you know what I'm like.
H: And the sun sets. Extinguished by a black veil.
K: Great. I've never felt hornier. You're gonna feel my tongue. And my cock.
    Hear me?
I: Crazy! You're something. Really something. You.
H: Air. Help! Help! From up there. Angels, swarms of angels. Myr-i-ads.
K: Cream! Oooh! The straight-jacket! Come on.
I: The pain. This pain. You're something.
K: Look at her choking. Slap my thigh! Fun-ny!
H: God near . . . to . . . oh . . . oh.
K: She's dying. Crazy.
I: Kiss me. You! Oh baby. Oh my big baby.
H: The universe! Co-lors.
K: (*Belly laugh.*)
I: Death.

## I+L–H

I: They used you for the freeze test?

H: (Nods.)

L: Turned out quite well in this case. I'd almost go as far as to say the specimen looks healthier than it did before.

I: Very interesting. Can you tell us what you experienced as you came around?

H: (Shakes head.)

L: Unfortunately this specimen had its vocal chords removed.

I: I see. What was the reason?

L: Well, when we chose it for the test it was extremely frightened. It was yelling so loudly it affected team-concentration.

I: Very interesting. Fear, yelling . . . almost human reactions.

L: Right. But with these specimens the oddest things occur.

I: My dear child, do you normally feel hungry at regular intervals?

H: (Shrugs shoulders.)

L: You can almost set your clock by it. A decidedly punctual drive to take nourishment.

I: Yes. And the bowels?

L: Yes, this specimen in particular also has a decidedly regular pattern of bowel movements. Very little maintenance necessary. You can't say that for all of them.

I: One final question. Did the heat treatment give any reason to hope for a future pregnancy?

L: To our regret, unfortunately not. For several reasons the specimen appears to be sterile.


IAN: Here is the picture, taken shortly before his death.

MYRA: Gives the impression of an animal. As an adult he'd have been a cipher.

IAN: No question. Here he is dead.

MYRA: Peaceful expression on his face.

IAN: Confirms it. For inferior creatures death means happiness. And for the worthy, life.

MYRA: Few are blessed with your clarity of thought.

IAN: You're right, Hessie. Start the tape. I'd like to hear for a second time just how an animal transforms once again into an animal. Ours is the integrity and the will to correct Nature's errors. (Taped scene of John Killbridge's death.) You can hear him whine.

MYRA: I hear it. Not like your voice—clear and direct. We are pure and clean. Not like the inferior creatures.

IAN: Still, it all went too fast. Another experiment will be conducted. Is the rent paid?

MYRA: I took care of it.

IAN: Buy barbed wire. The next experiment must be with a female subject. She will be bound with barbed wire. Try to get some that's old and rusty.

\*\*\*

A: When Jesus beheld the cross, he reached out his bleeding arms to it with great longing, kissed it and embraced it with all his heart and placed it on his bruised shoulders. Although he was at death's door, he did indeed rejoice and go his way in greatness.

B: Holy Mary, Mother of God, bless me so that I may share in your suffering. Enkindle my heart with pain that I may partake of your love.

C :
All the blows he must suffer
Debased and forced to bear his cross
All this and more to profit me.

\*\*\*

(*From the tape, sounds of a girl dying, and the lines . . .*) [*The next six lines English original.*]

MYRA: Make an end with her now.

IAN: Ok. Ok. Just a moment.

MYRA: All up with her?

IAN: Easily done.

MYRA: There is no gasp anymore.

IAN: Now she is gone.

IAN: Hessie, your eyes. They are more and more like steel. Bluer than blue.

MYRA: You have helped me to become myself. It *is* taking effect, isn't it?

IAN: Yes, Hessie. It is. Especially your body. The muscle tone. You are achieving nobility. I am pleased.

MYRA: To hear that from you is divine. It is.

IAN: Yes, Hessie. The time has come to spread the doctrine. Do you agree?

MYRA: Certainly. It must happen. This great thing must be carried forth. Those who are sacrificed will be as a tidal wave. And they will be grateful.

IAN: I suggest we keep to blood relatives. My cousin you are acquainted with. He will be Bormann. It will take real effort to initiate him to the perfection of our thought.

MYRA: No effort will be too great to carry forth your ideas. None.

IAN: It will happen. Indoctrination sessions will be arranged in the evenings.

MYRA: Good. Your ideas are of such magnitude that they will be grasped quickly. Isn't that so?

IAN: It is. However, it will be difficult for everyone to understand the ultimate consequences. Even blood relations will find it hard.

MYRA: I have the greatest trust in your blood relations. The ideas will flow through the blood. Isn't that so?

IAN: It must be. Nothing that is similar to me can be inferior. It is.

# H+K-I

K: Ya had someone in again last night.

I: That's my business.

K: It ain't your business. Accordin' to the law.

H: If it happens again, you get notice.

K: Yeah, that's how it is, cuz we ain't interested in being liable. Get that through your thick skull.

I: Who's going to pay you a hundred and fifty for a room like this where you can't even have a little privacy.

H: You watch your smart mouth! I called your company to see if you were still working there. What do you think they told me?

I: What?

H: That you ain't been on the job for three weeks.

K: So how do you make your living now? Or don't you want us to know?

I: Do I ask you how well you're shitting in the toilet?

H: Ok that's it! On the first you're out. You got your notice, definite.

K: After the first we don't want to see you.

I: Yeah sure, but I get my deposit back at least.

H: Don't talk crap. We're covered in ways you can only dream about. That is, if you're not too far gone even to dream about it.

K: I don't even wanna know what's gonna become of her.

# I+L-M

I: Why did you spread that stuff around about us?

L: You think it's right they're all talking about us?

M: That's just how people talk.

L: No, not "just how people talk."—I hold you responsible. I could kick your ass for this.

.: Sounds good to me. Kick away.

L: Real good.

I: Do it, go ahead.

L: Maybe. What about you? Got a better idea?

M: What do you mean?

L: Something. You better believe it.

M: I don't understand a word of what you're saying.

L: Then think it over. Just consider it a second. No idea? Nothing? How about now?

M: Just tell me for chrissake. What do you mean?

L: I'm thinking of a little settlement. Geetus. Ca-ash.

I: Brilliant. You're brilliant.
M: I don't have any money. Not much anyhow.
L: But that little you have. You will of course turn that over voluntarily. To make up for the personal damages you've caused.
I: Move, pal. The wallet.
M: Ok. Twenty bucks.
L: Twenty bucks?
M: Yeah. Or what?
I: Now *you* can give him a little encouragement.

L+M-K

M: You're my friend. I've already been in India, Nepal, almost got to China.
L: What about Norway, Finland? The North is great. Finnish women.
M: I dig the South.
L: Hey look at that one. Some belly! And a carnation in his buttonhole.
M: Shoe leather—two hundred meters, max! Then it's strictly BMWs and the elevator scene.
K: I eat whatever I feel like. Because I work. Telephoning makes you hungry. Fresh air can give you an appetite too.
M: Check out your cheeks. Son of Hamster!
K: Like I said I work for my cheeks.
M: Hamsters'd dig you, pal.
K: Because I'm on my own, nowhere to hang out. If I had someplace, the picture'd be different. Completely different.
L: This kick in your shins makes me happy.
M: What makes me happy is beating on your head.
L: And this uppercut to your chin.
M: And this left hook to your spleen.
L: Breaking bones.
M: The kind with bellies attached.
K: Let me buy you a beer.
M: Now that sounds better. In fact much better.
L: Let's go. Beer city!

IAN BRADY IV

She grew totally apathetic and for months wore only black. Everyone was to blame for the doll's death. She herself was an excellent swimmer but on that afternoon was too lazy to go to the pond. Duke, grandmother's dog, became her new favorite, until he got run over by a car. Grandma said that was too bad and bought herself a new dog. Myra dressed in black again. First she wanted to enter a convent and take the veil, but instead she took to the hair dryer. Sometimes blond, sometimes with a little red in her hair, full of stilted expressions from women's magazines, and untouchable to the boys in the neighbor-hood, she waited for the one she knew would come. From the very first moment she knew Ian Brady was it. But Ian Brady paid no attention to the busty, long-legged girl. To be more precise: for months he subjected her to an ordeal of alternating hope and despair. An encouraging look would be followed by weeks of indifference; a few words tossed her way, by weeks of silence. He ignored her at lunch and beavered away at his German. He read *Mein Kampf*, por-nographic literature, *The Kiss of the Whip*, and mysteries. When he had a cold, Myra wrote in her diary, "I'd love to take care of him."

L+M−H

L: Nice piece of cunt.
M: Horny piece of cunt.
L: Let's fuck her.
M: Gotta do it. Now.
H: No, please don't.
L: Heel, bitch. Don't we turn you on?
H: If you don't let me go, I'll scream. (*Screams.*)
M: Scream away, cunt. Nobody's gonna hear you.
H: Please, please. Let me go.
L: Oooh, makes us hot when you yell like that. Go ahead, yell.
H: Help! Help!
M: Ha. Yeah. Hold her arms tight.
L: Right.
H: Mommy! Mommy!
M: You can yell for mommy all you want.
L: I wish she *was* here. Then we'd have one apiece.
M: You dirty slut, don't scratch me. You *do* want it, don't you? Admit
   it. Ow! What are you, crazy?
L: Yeah, she's crazy.
H: No kissing. Please, no kissing.
L: Why not? Don't you like my mouth? I brushed them this morning. Just like
   you're supposed to.
M: Ok, no fooling now. Hold her arms. Still got your cherry, sister? I'm gonna
   carve it up with my little knife.
L: It's nice, honey. Believe me, real nice.

H+K−L

K: We gotta talk. Serious. About d'future.
H: Don't be too strick wit'm. He ain't all there.
L: You tellin' me I'm not all there.

H: Come on, just a little, you know. Slow, but he's ok.

K: It don' interest me. I wanna know about the money angle. The pocketbook, nothin' else.

L: What's he mean?

H: How much a week you make? Whatta ya got in the bank? That kinda thing.

L: Hundred eighty a week. Gross. Nine hundred twenty in the bank. Franklin Savings and Loan.

K: You gonna keep a woman on that? You oughta be ashamed.

L: S'gonna get betta.

K: A wet fart maybe, but money that ain't. Blush! Go ahead! Cause you should be embarrassed.

H: That ain't too much, I guess, yeah.

K: You serious all of a sudden? About him?

L: No kiddin'. S'gonna get betta.

K: Betta, worse. That kinda money it don' make no difference.

H: But the physical thing—you know—that's pretty good.

K: Then stick to the physical, and drop them other ideas.

## H+L−I

L: Now that is one beautiful girl.

I: That one?

L: Yeah. Yeah. You know her?

I: Sure. Come over here you.

H: You want something from me?

L: How much you get?

H: What's it worth to you?

L: Well . . . I don't know.

H: You have to say.

L: Fifty?

H: Ok.

I: But you picked me.

L: Yeah, before.

I: That's not right.

L: Look, I'll pay you anyway. Ok?

I: Yeah, sure.

L: God, you are beautiful.

H: Oh?

L: Yeah, and you know it.

H: Maybe so.

L: You turn me on. You here a lot?

H: I work here.

L: But I've never seen you.

H: Yeah. I always go quick.
L: I guess so. Should we go?
H: Sure. The sooner the better.
L: Right. See you.
H: Bye now. Be happy, hear!
I: Yeah, but being happy ain't always fun.
***

IAN: The girl was tougher than the boy. Strange, really strange.

MYRA: Possibly descended from a marginally superior race. The barbed wire caused her a great deal of pain, yet she never once begged for mercy.

IAN: Still, there was fear in her eyes. Did you see it, Hessie? Did you?

MYRA: Certainly. But hunger affected her first. When I held the piece of bread in front of her eyes, they crossed. Did you see it, my Führer, did you?

IAN: I did. Certainly. Though I was scrutinizing the subject for possible signs of shame. But the thing is beyond any feeling of shame. It is. It was.

MYRA: Yes. Strange. Certainly. We'll have to make a note of that. Inferiority of a creature's race corresponds to diminished natural feelings of shame.

IAN: It almost drove me into a temper. Before my eyes a naked creature—and no effort made to cover the place between its legs. My anger at the thought of this kind of thing—supposedly with the same right to life as the higher beings in our civilization. It nearly made me forget our plan to make the experiment last longer. It did.

MYRA: I commend your self-restraint.

IAN: I thank you, Myra.

MYRA: Surely this type has no God!? I can answer the question myself. No.

IAN: Make notes and I'll check them. We will have to build upon this.
***

C: Peace be with you. By what name shall the child be called?
A: Alfred.
C: Alfred, what do you desire from the Church of God?
A: Faith.
C: What does faith grant you?
A: Eternal life.
C: And so if you seek eternal life you must obey these commandments:
    Thou shalt love the Lord thy God
    With thy whole heart
    With thy whole soul
    And with thy whole mind
    And love thy neighbor as thyself.
A,B: We renounce the devil and all his works and deeds.
A,B,C: (Singing.)
    True to our bond may I ever remain
    The church and her word will I heed.
***

MYRA: Therefore all inferior life is to be eliminated. You understand.

JIMMY: Ok. Sure.

IAN: That's not something people just say. There are conclusions to be drawn. Direct conclusions.

MYRA: Quite direct. You understand?

JIMMY: Yeah, but . . .

MYRA: Ok, one more time. Even the unworthy need breathing room, living space. But they do not have a right to it. That's in the nature of the unworthy. Isn't it?

JIMMY: Yeah. Anyhow. So?

IAN: You must draw a conclusion from that.

MYRA: Have you drawn a conclusion?

JIMMY: (Nods.) No.

MYRA: I'll explain it another way. You want to lie down in your bed. But someone is in it. What do you do?

JIMMY: I kick him out. That's what.

IAN: That's the point.

MYRA: There are many creatures on this planet who are breathing your air. Who are walking on streets which belong to you, not them. And what are you doing to them? What should you be doing?

JIMMY: Kicking them out. That's it. Kick them out.

IAN: That is precisely our task. To kick out the unworthy. It must be.

JIMMY: But how?

MYRA: I'll bet you have a friend who is worthless. See, get him over here, we'll show you how. We will.

## H + K – M

H: The boy made indecent advances toward me. It was blatant. Normally I don't get this way. You know me. I'm liberal with young people. Everyone knows that. But there are limits.

K: How did it happen?

H: It was shower-time. I suppose you know the new grouping puts the young ones in the shower together with the sixteen to eighteen year olds. Much as I regret to say it, young people don't really scrub themselves without supervision. And then, oh how horrible . . .

K: Stop crying, dear. What did you do to her to upset her like this?

H: He has to be punished. Punish him! The parents must be informed. Who knows? We may have a potential sex fiend here.

K: That's correct. In these matters we can't be careful enough. What can you say in your own defense? What did you do to her?

H: He's being stubborn. Incredible. I would like to stress how this ties in with his schoolwork. It's been sliding. What happened doesn't really surprise me.

K: How interesting. So your academic work leaves something to be desired too. The schoolboy lust is no big surprise then.

H: He reached under my sweater and grabbed my breast.

K: I thought it was something like that. The incident must be reported to his parents. People like to know what they're raising.

H: And spending their money on. And denying themselves for.

K: People like to know. And your parents are sure to be interested in this little episode.

H: I'm sure of that.

## K+L−M

K: Who shit his pants and crammed them in the toilet? Mr. Pisser and Moaner! That's who. Clear as day.

L: The toilet's stuffed up. He jerked off last night too. Bedstains. I saw them.

K: Mister Pisser and Moaner! And pigged up the shithouse walls with all kinds of graffiti. And who messed up the table—the slob did the job, that's who.

M: [*English original.*] Hand in hand. Hand in it. It in it. That's it.

K: (*Contra publico.*) Did you jerk off last night?

L: I don't care about them. But he's different. I know all about him.

K: That sort of graffiti undermines the men's morale. A pocketknife! Do you have a pocketknife?

L: Yes.

K: On the ground. Opened. Ready for action.

L: Laying and ready. Ready to cut.

K: Corporal Markus!

M: Reporting!

K: You know the game! Push-ups over open weapon.

M: At your command, sir.

K: Men like us need kicks, and when we need them we get them. Men like us— we're on the way. We're gonna be all that we can be.

L: Seven. Eight. Nine. Ten.

H, I: (*To those doing push-ups.*) [*English original.*] I wanna be loved by you.

## K+L−H

K: But you were friends.

H: You know that already.

L: When did you last see him?

H: Last week, Wednesday or Thursday.

L: And where did you meet him?

H: In a café. I think it was the Capri.

K: This pistol! Is it yours?

H: Yes.
K: He was shot with this pistol.
H: I didn't do anything. It wasn't me. Leave me alone.
L: When was the last time you saw the pistol?
H: A month ago. Maybe two.
K: Didn't you notice it was lost?
H: Maybe.
L: And why didn't you report it?
H: It didn't seem that important.
K: Why did you murder him?
H: It wasn't me. Why would I want to murder him? It wasn't me.
L: Let's just say—jealousy.
H: I could never be jealous of him.
L: Talk! We asked you a question.
K: Out with it! Why didn't you report the lost weapon?
L: Why did you shoot him?
K: Where were you last night between two and three?
L: Didn't he promise to marry you?
K: Out with it! Talk! You're not dealing with children here.

## IAN BRADY V

The cold-shoulder treatment lasted until the beginning of 1962, when he arrived for a New Year's Eve party: a man of the world, button-hole perfect and
goose-stepping, with a bottle of German wine under his arm. Myra's parents
were charmed by him, Myra was plastered when he brought her home to
grandma's house. They snuck into Myra's room and Ian got right to the point.
He deflowered her at once, mercilessly, and left as if nothing had happened. At
home, always within easy reach in the closet, lay his picture of Irm Grese, the
real power behind the commandant of the Bergen-Belsen concentration camp.
Myra must have a Dirndl made for herself, the Teutonic woman is perfect and
is given the name Hessie, after Rudolf Hess, deputy to the Führer. Every night
they drink German wine and listen to the German Führer on American
records, *Hitler's Inferno*. Myra goes to buy bottles of wine, more each time—two,
three, then four—but during the day at the office no one notices they're a couple. And then Ian Brady began to take photgraphs. First a few pictures of
Hessie on the moors, then Hessie in bed. Bookkeeper Brady carries sexy lingerie
home in his briefcase. At first Myra doesn't want to wear it. Then she does,
urged on by Ian and his little leather whip. The whip and Myra's striped
backside can be seen in one of the thirty photographs confiscated by the police.

## H+I−K

H: How much so far today?

I: Fifty.

H: Not bad. What's *he* want? Are you nuts?

K: What do you mean? I have rights too.

H: This here ain't no place for faggots.

I: You want to mess up our business?

K: Don't bug me, you'll be better off.

H: Perverts screw up our image around here.

K: Come off it, honey. Once they see my ass, you're in for a bull market.

H: Asses are for grabbing, that's all.

K: Not mine.

L: Ok beat it. Or I call the boss.

K: Is he the hot and horny type?

I: What's it to you, shithead? He ain't nothing.

K: Come off it, sweetie. I just want to know if he has a dick, a wild and crazy dick. That's the kind I dream about. Every night.

H: Christ is this one sick!

I: Ever got it on with a woman?

K: Come off it, do I look like a lesbian? Hmmm? Not for me, thanks.

I: Fucking fags, makes you puke.

H: The fairy brotherhood.

I: Loving brothers.

H: Get the fuck out of here anyhow.

K+M−L

K: How was Little Rock? I mean the car race. How much did you make?

L: You know, not bad. It's a living.

M: Some job you pulled too, huh!!!

L: What job? What are you talking about?

K: We just want to know who was boss. The boss, get it? Hummm? Talk!

L: Ow! I . . . hey, ow . . . I don't know the names. There were two of them.

M: Let him go.

L: There was a woman too.

M: Was it Myra?

K: See. Ok.

M: Where are they? Both of them.

L: They screwed me. Like all the rest.

K: Use your head. Go ahead.

M: How does the cigarette taste like this?

K: Tell us, darling. Then we'll be real nice.

M: Stubborn little bastard.

K: Be nice.

L: She owns a bar in Dallas. Now quit it!

M: Sweetheart Myra, a bar in Dallas. What do you know.

L: I didn't get anything. Nothing.

M: Let's get on with it.

K: Ok.

L: What are you going to do? No. No. (*Boot.*) Hey! You didn't have to do that. I wouldn't have told . . .

M: Poor rat. Tiny little rat.

## H+I−M

H: I'm a charter member of SAFF. If that makes you drool it's your own fault.

I: S-A-F-F: Sexual Activity Fast and Frequent.

H: Fuckyourself, as they say in the USA. That's what I say to you.

I: God knows there are better looking men.

H: And better in bed.

I: Has he even got one?

H: Not very big, as far as I can tell.

I: Hair on his chest?

H: Not much. Sweet ass though. I'd be happy if he'd just lie on his belly. Real sweet ass. As for the rest . . .

M: Why are you turning on me? You said it was like God's angels singing in heaven. And the way you moaned, and sweat like a pig. You.

H: I know what the guys with little weenies want. They want to feel like Tarzan.

I: (*Laughs.*)

H: Basically I prefer foreign cock to the domestic variety. Some of them though —wink and they come. All over themselves.

I: Did you screw the one with the eagles on his chest?

H: Wow! Talk about a humping machine!

M: (*Groans, moans.*)

H: Oh, yeah. Moan away. On the high wire without a net. But the decisions— they've been made.

M: Think it over. I'll give you three days.

H: (*Laughter, clear as a bell.*)

***

JIMMY: I feel sick. The way he's lying there. And he's dead. Real dead.

IAN: We will take him to the moor tomorrow. We will.

JIMMY: He's so dead.

MYRA: He robbed your air. And your space. And he was worthless.

IAN: Pull yourself together. My blood pulses through your veins. Be hard.

JIMMY: I have to try.

MYRA: Right. You don't want us to find you unworthy. That you don't want.

JIMMY: No.

IAN: Right, so pull yourself together! You are still inadequate in many areas.

Strength, courage, utter purity. You will have to become a master.

JIMMY: The way he screamed.

MYRA: Because he was unworthy. Very unworthy. The worthy remain silent and are worthy. And that is not certain. Their silence doesn't mean they're worthy. We decide who is worthy.

IAN: You too shall be one of those who may decide. You shall. You must become a master. A master over life and death.

MYRA: Go home now. Consider what you have learned today. It will give you strength. It will help you. Now go. And never forget that you must become like us.

***

Cast off the old man and take on the new. Be a worthy sacrifice to thy Lord, purified not only through the blood of rams and calves, but through the blood of Christ. Eat of his flesh and drink of his blood and thou shalt live for all eternity.

## K+M−I

M: Fun? Walking the streets?

I: It's ok.

K: Real fucking pigs, whores. Man-crazy pigs.

I: No one's making you do it.

K: You bet your ass. Not me.

M: How much you get?

I: Thirty for a trick in a car. Hotel costs fifty.

M: So? You any good?

I: Front and back, in the mouth. Whatever your heart desires.

K: Fucking pig.

I: Kiss my ass.

M: He ain't all wrong. Considering you do it with everyone.

I: All sorts of cock—big, small, washed, unwashed.

M: Don't you whores spread disease?

I: Just the opposite. We get regular check-ups, us.

K: So you think you're worth fifty?

I: Depends what you like.

K: I wouldn't waste two marks on her. Not me.

I: On your wife you would. That's what she gets, right? And she's better, huh?

K: Shut up about my wife.

M: His wife. There's a respectable woman. Nothing doing with her.

I: I'm respectable too. In my way. And honest.

K: You honest? With your eyes, and that face?

I: In my heart's where I'm respectable.

K: Don't make me laugh.

## I+K–H

H: Desire, wild and rapturous. The soul shudders. (*Epileptic fit. Continuous.*)
K: I sent for the ambulance.
H: Grey shadows in front of my lids. Lemons and hyacinths.
I: Cut the crap.
K: Let her alone. I can see her arms in the straight-jacekt already, and it makes me squirm. But out of pure lust.
I: You!
K: Right. Now you know what I'm like.
H: And the sun sets. Extinguished by a black veil.
K: Great. I've never felt hornier. You're going to feel my tongue. And my cock. Hear me?
I: Crazy! You're something. Really something. You.
H: Air. Help! Help! From up there. Angels, swarms of angels. Myr-i-ads.
K: Cream! Ooh! The straight-jacket! Come on.
I: The pain. This pain. You're something.
K: Look at her choking. Slap my thigh! Fun-ny!
H: God near . . . to . . . oh . . . oh.
K: She's dying. Crazy.
I: Kiss me. You! Oh baby. Oh my big baby.
H: The universe! Co-lors.
K: (*Belly laugh.*)
I: Death.

## I+L–H

I: They used you for the freeze test?
H: (*Nods.*)
L: Turned out quite well in this case. I'd almost go as far as to say the specimen looks healthier now than it did before.
I: Very interesting. Can you tell us what you experienced as you came around.
L: Unfortunately this specimen had its vocal chords removed.
I: I see. What was the reason?
L: Well, when we chose it for the test it was extremely frightened. It was yelling so loudly it affected team concentration.
I: Very interesting. Fear, yelling . . . almost human reactions.
L: Right. But with these specimens the oddest things occur.
I: My dear child, do you normally feel hungry at regular intervals?
H: (*Shrugs shoulders.*)
L: You can almost set your clock by it. A decidedly punctual drive to take nourishment.
I: Yes. And the bowels?

L: Yes, this specimen in particular also has a decidedly regular pattern of bowel movements. Very little maintenance necessary. You can't say that for all of them.

I: One final question. As heat spread through the specimen were there any signs of the possibility of future pregnancy?

L: To our regret, unfortunately not. For several reasons the specimen appears to be sterile.

## IAN BRADY VI

Ian can be seen too, alone and with Myra during intercourse, then both again with Ku Klux Klan hoods over their heads or with blasé looks on their faces. Life speeds us—movies, then wine, then sex, and the same in reverse order. The Nürnberg trials, the Satan of the Night and a few bottles of Liebfraumilch in a rented car somewhere on the moors. Life acquires direction once again when by pure chance Ian buys a book which both fascinates and has a calming effect on him. It is *Justine, or the Misfortunes of Virtue* by the Marquis de Sade. They both read the book. He points out the key sentence to her: "What I need is an intelligent, good looking woman who has already gone the way of pain herself; in a single word, an efficient young woman devoid of pity who knows exactly what she wants." Myra knows what she wants when after a booze-up on the moor she drives Ian in the rented car past the market in Ashton under Lyne. It is 5:45 p.m. In the fog a boy is leaning on a garbage can. The car stops. John Killbridge gets in.

\*\*\*

# APPENDIX
**The following four liturgical passages were used only in the Munich and (identical) Darmstadt productions.**

A., B., C.

Blood and Wine
Wine and Blood
Blood to Wine
Wine to Blood
Blood to Blood
Blood is Wine
Wine is Blood
Bloodwine
MYRA: [*English original.*] Bloody God ff.
IAN: Calix sanguinis tuis ff.

A., B., C.

And Jesus being full of the Holy Ghost returned from Jordan, and was led by the Spirit into the wilderness, and was tempted by the devil.

(Luke 4, 1)

***

Thou mighty Virgin
Thou art the mirror of justice
Thou art the source of our joy
Thou art the chalice of the Spirit
Thou mystic rose
Thou ivory tower
Thou golden mansion
Thou ark of the covenant
Thou gate of heaven
Thou morning star
Pray for us ff

***

A: (*Sings.*) Lamb of God I thirst for thy blood.
B: He hangs there stripped and naked.
C: Behold his wounds.
B: His head is bowed.
C: His heart pierced.
B: Arms outstretched.
C: Oh what love.

The order of scenes in the Munich premiere was precisely symmetrical:


6 contres
1 narration
4 contres
1 narration
3 contres
(*Regularly alternating*)
1 pas des deux
1 liturgical passage
thus nine times
(*Then reprise of the contres in reverse order with the remaining narrations*)
2 contres
1 narration
3 contres
1 narration
4 contres
1 narration
6 contres

*** 

Exact order of the Munich premiere:


They used you for the freeze test?
We gotta talk.
Why did you spread that stuff around about us?
Fun? Walking the streets?
Desire, wild and rapturous
Now that is one beautiful girl.
Ian Brady I.
Nice piece of cunt.
The boy made indecent advances toward me.
You're my friend.
How was Little Rock?
Ian Brady II.
But you were friends.
I'm a charter member of SAFF.
How much so far today?
Ian Brady III.
Ya had someone in again last night.
Who shit his pants and crammed them in the toilet?
I'm coming to your party tonight.

Despise this world . . .
I showed you the photographs.
  Blood and wine . . .
You know why I had to hit you.
  And Jesus being full of the Holy Ghost . . .
You behaved as I've come to expect.
  God's will is supreme . . .
Here is the picture, taken shortly before his death.
  When Jesus beheld the cross . . .
Hessie, your eyes.
  Peace be with you . . .
The girl was tougher than the boy.
  Thou mighty Virgin . . .
Therefore all inferior life is to be eliminated.
  Lamb of God . . .
I feel sick. The way he's lying there.
  Cast off the old man . . .
Who shit his pants and crammed them in the toilet?
Ya had someone in again last night.
Ian Brady IV.
How much so far today?
I'm a charter member of SAFF.
But you were friends.
Ian Brady V.
How was Little Rock?
You're my friend.
The boy made indecent advances toward me.
Nice piece of cunt.
Ian Brady VI.
Now that is one beautiful girl.
Desire, wild and rapturous.
Fun? Walking the streets?
Why did you spread that stuff around about us?
We gotta talk.
They used you for the freeze test?

# Garbage, The City and Death

CHARACTERS:

Roma B.
Fräulein Emma von Waldenstein
Fräulein Tau
Asbach-Lilly
Miss Violet
Marie-Antoinette
Achfeld
Kraus, Peter
Müller II
Franz B.
The Little Prince
Hans von Gluck
Oscar von Leiden
Hellfritz, Tenor
Jim
The Rich Jew
The Dwarf
Herr Müller
Frau Müller

# PART ONE

## Scene 1

*On the moon, because it is just as uninhabitable as the earth, especially the cities. Down left, wrapped in plastic: Marie Antoinette and Jim. Roma B., Fräulein Emma von Waldenstein, Fräulein Tau, Asbach-Lilly and Miss Violet are eating breakfast. At the same time they are waiting for customers.*

FRL. TAU & MISS VIOLET: (*In a round.*)
Evening's silence now has paled,
Yet by th' creek a nightingale,
In her sweet manner sings,
Lamenting through the Vale.

FRL. EMMA: You should have given him up.

ASBACH-LILLY: On account of that filthy bourgeois sow! Come on! She sticks him up her pussy and he disappears. Speechless. Not even a gleam in his eye.

ROMA B.: How's a gleam in his eye gonna help him in a jail cell?

FRL. EMMA: And when they let him out he'll break her head. You should have given him up. But then, we're bourgeois too. At least in our souls.

ASBACH-LILLY: My soul is mine, Fräulein von Waldenstein. No one's going to have an easy time laying his grubby hands on it.

ROMA B.: The soul is God's property, Fraulein, not yours. A loan, so to speak. You put yourself up for hire. That's Good. You get paid. You're one of us: a whore. Smiling? Don't smile. It can so easily make you look stupid.

FRL. EMMA: He'll get two years. Three at the most. That works on a man, works on him and grows in him until he explodes. The blast will teach us fear.

ASBACH-LILLY: You're scaring me, Fräulein von Waldenstein. And you like scaring me. You're sick. It was a fatal night, that's true. Desire in my flesh, my skull filled with hate, the loud mournful cry of my womb. Your cock, Oscar, give it to me. Your cock. You know—surely—that Oscar is one of nature's wonders. Now we're both shrivelling up.

ROMA B.: You feel sorry for yourself, betray the man, feel sorry for yourself on account of the betrayed man. You wait too long to use your brains.

*(Achfeld comes. Places himself in the middle of the prostitutes and counts off.)*

ACHFELD:
Eeeni, meeni, mini, mo, I'll fuck you in the toe,
Eeeni, meeni, mini, mu, the hole belongs to you. *(It's Miss Violet. She gets up and leaves with Achfeld.)*

FRL. TAU: His cock is so small he could safely fuck her in the ear.

ASBACH-LILLY: I don't know, this cold between moist sheets. And the sheets are always moist. Only Oscar understood to dry them. He performed wonders. But he lied to me.

FRL. EMMA: A healthy lie is like fresh early morning dew.

ROMA B.: But look, what would truth be without lies? Lies themselves.

*(Kraus, Peter, Müller II and Franz B. slowly cross the stage. They pull their pistols and shoot Asbach-Lilly. It is a symbolic act. Asbach-Lilly spins about in the air and screams. Then she collapses. The three men go, as they came. Silence.)*

FRL. TAU: *(Sings.)* Evening's silence. . . . *(The others join in. Asbach-Lilly wakes up again.)*

ASBACH-LILLY: My God that's beautiful. Dying.

FRL. TAU: It looked fairly genuine. You should take some more classes.

ASBACH-LILLY: It was fear I had in my gut.

FRL. TAU: So fear is good for acting?

ASBACH-LILLY: Apparently. I knew it would only be blanks. After all, we're not in Chicago. *(The Little Prince comes quickly.)*

LITTLE PRINCE: Excuse me. I'm in a hurry. My nerves. Well, my boss you understand, this rich Jew, most of you know him of course, oh to have such a head! Within the next half hour he wants—is there method in his madness, you ask yourself—one with hefty breasts, those are his words, not tits, he said, not a set of lungs, no, breasts, as though it were a mother he wanted to find for himself *(Frl. Tau stands up and leaves with him)*, a mother, who he conjures up in his brain, shoving a fist into her face and licking her hefty, sagging tits. If you have money, madness will soon follow. I always say that to comfort myself, you'll excuse me. We can chat another time. *(The Little*

*Prince and Frl. Tau have gone. Silence.*)

ROMA B.: It's peaceful when no one is singing.

ASBACH-LILLY: Would be if you didn't keep gabbing.

FRL. EMMA: Oh please don't, please don't fight. That always makes me so sad.

ROMA B.: For your sake the world will unfold itself. But—you're right. And that's sure to pay off.

ASBACH-LILLY: I've been especially enjoying my food since that man can no longer take away my appetite.

ROMA B.: Might be so. If it weren't that hunger devours itself. Like thoughts. It's dark, and there's a trembling inside my skull. (*Hans von Gluck enters and sings "The Little Night Music." Asbach-Lilly stands up and dances to the music. The pair exit, dancing and singing.*)

ROMA B.: Do you know the fable of the grinning Chinaman?

FRL. EMMA: No.

ROMA B.: Me neither. But I'm sure there is one. Because everything exists. The world is small, and thoughts, the countless thoughts which have been thought will bring it to its teetering edge. And one day it will briefly shudder and come crashing in on itself. And the thoughts, the hideous ones and the beautiful, will become nothing—be nothing and everything. As meaningless as now.

FRL. EMMA: You are mean, Roma, you're making fun, and inside you triumph over me. You want to win, to win, and this victory brings you the warmth you need, and I freeze to death in your omnipotence.

ROMA B.: Don't think. Thoughts kill pleasure. (*Oscar von Leiden enters slowly.*)

OSCAR: I'm afraid. I was always afraid of women. I won't ever touch one, I think, never. Then their penetrating rays can't affect me. But that's not true. I dream that I can elude death by avoiding the touch of a woman. Then the thoughts clash. And they both lead to death. An idea blitzes through my head: I'll choose death by woman . . . Yes, I'll be the victim of the executioner, of women. I'll take the brunette. The blonde is all—crystal. She'll shatter and I'll cut myself. I can't stand blood. (*Oscar von Leiden and Frl. Emma leave. Roma B. begins to sing the round but then abruptly stops.*)

ROMA B.: It's cold. And Franz needs money. (*Hellfritz, Tenor enters. Today he is a Turkish street cleaner. He rummages through the remains of the whores's breakfast.*)

ROMA B.: Love?

HELLFRITZ, TENOR: Love? Love no.

ROMA B.: Ten marks. Five! Hate!

HELLFRITZ, TENOR: Hate good—better than love. Love no good. Much love, much sickness. (*He leaves.*)

ROMA B.: Beat it, you filthy migrant dick, you stinking mangy dog, you puke, you monster, you—man! (*She takes her knife, screams the word "Men," runs moaning and groaning to the plastic mass, stabs it, blood comes out. The plastic*

*comes apart, Marie-Antoinette and Jim step out of the plastic, they are naked.*)
MARIE-ANTOINETTE & JIM: (*Duet from La Traviata. Roma kneels in prayer. Behind her the set is being shifted.*)

## Scene 2

(*Kitchen in an apartment, realistic. Franz B. comes in the door.*)

FRANZ B.: Now?

ROMA B.: Don't hit.

FRANZ B.: Who hits you? The one who loves you hits you. So? Who hits you?

ROMA B.: You—love me, so. . . .

FRANZ B.: So I hit you if I love you. But I can't love you all day long and all night long. And then all day long again. How much?

ROMA B.: (*Stands up.*)

FRANZ B.: So? How much?! I get it. Nothing again. That's the third time this week.

ROMA B.: It was cold, Franz. My legs were turning to stone. I did gymnastics, deep breathing. Finally even prayed. It was hours. No one came. Like a jinx.

FRANZ B.: And now? How do I look? Can I let myself be seen with the rest of them, the successful ones? Can I drink a beer in good conscience: won't the others notice me, failure pasted on my brow?

ROMA B.: I beg your forgiveness.

FRANZ B.: What's your forgiveness to me? To die in humility like this is miserable. Give me freedom, Roma, and freedom is money. It's Saturday, the bank's closed. The racetrack awaits. I must do what I must do. Go. Work. Quickly and successfully. And produce!

ROMA B.: It's cold, Franz. My knees tremble. I cough. For days I've been coughing. This coughing is scary. I wanted to go to the doctor, but I had no money.

FRANZ B.: I will not be bargained with. I'll wait two hours, then I'll fetch you. So that your meekness can pass.

ROMA B.: I could ask Miss Violet, or the fat one. Just this cold, please understand.

FRANZ B.: I want to play with earned money, borrowed brings me no luck. You know that. And you talk and talk and time passes by and works against you.

ROMA B.: I know you're right. You're right and kind, and you hit me as little as possible, and forgive me my sins. I know all that. But the cold, Franz, it burns the fuzz from my skin. I'll be like a plucked chicken, pawning my gold teeth. Who do I cry to for help?

FRANZ B.: They dump on you because you're skinny. You have to eat. They pay you according to your weight. I've been saying that for years. But—are you listening to me?

ROMA B.: I'm listening to you. When you speak I listen to you, and late at night when you're sleeping I try to interpret your very breath.

FRANZ B.: Is that how well you know me?

ROMA B.: I know you. And where I know you you don't frighten me. But the dark thoughts, the strange feelings, what can someone like me understand about these things. That frightens me, a lot.

FRANZ B.: And without fear your kind couldn't live. Fear, it keeps you warm, alive. Without fear you are cheeky, insolent, and lazy. And the dead, Roma, don't cry. Now go. Do well and don't leave him in the lurch, the one who is there for you as you need him. Go, little one, go and let yourself be fucked. Do not forget the rubbers, nor the time I have given you. And be righteous. Men too are only human.

(*Scene change. "Liebestod," Tristan and Isolde. Asbach-Lilly and Hellfritz, Tenor dance.*)

## Scene 3

(*Street corner. Frl. Emma von Waldenstein is working. Roma B. comes. They kiss.*)

FRL. EMMA: What now? So he's not sympathetic.

ROMA B.: No. He begged me to try it again.

FRL. EMMA: That's love for you—that's it exactly. Where's the justice? Who's got the upper hand? Where you look for it and where you find it. (*Müller II comes—*)

ROMA B.: Hey, little guy! How'd you like both of us? You can do it without a rubber, honey, it's nice, believe me. Real nice. (*—and goes again.*) Despair—call it by its proper name, that'll raise you capital.

FRL. EMMA: Or get your skull bashed in, and your puss. Things are the way they are, so they say, and that's good: And your own despair is none at all, or it's cheap. For sale. They'll buy and sell anything. Suspenders, or souls which don't belong to them.

ROMA B.: "Stay: an hour and a half." Then he hits me, as he loves me, hits me, and I think if I had learned to enjoy the pain I'd enjoy the blows and love would be love, which it isn't.

FRL. EMMA: I'll lend you my fur, honey. You're freezing.

ROMA B.: And asks me, what was the cock like, Roma, big or little? Did he last a while or come quick? Did he moan, he wants to know, use names—I've forgotten, I say, to me it wasn't important. There's a crash and stars twinkle in the firmament. And I learn to let myself get fucked fully conscious, eyes and ears open. What does he get out of it? He goes into the toilet and masturbates. Does he become a new man?

FRL. EMMA: No one is the way he is. Everyone's different. Who knows for sure. ( *Miss Violet comes.*)

MISS VIOLET: From day to day the city's getting bigger. The people in it are getting smaller and smaller.

ROMA B.: It's too cold. They stay home with their wives. Tell the children fairy tales about witches and wicked creatures.

MISS VIOLET: They cleaned up "The Tijuana Sunshine," arrested Rückert. There was a bank robbery. The place is cleaned out.

FRL. EMMA: And Gustav?

MISS VIOLET: I don't know anything for sure. Rumors, you know how it is. Whispers across the city, causing fear where fear is deserved. They have their methods alright, which kill where they should.

ROMA B.: I've been coughing for days. Not enough for the doctor this week. I'll take care of myself next week. Even if I still don't have enough I'll be happy. What do I expect him to say? I'm healthy. Then it's wasted money. And if I'm dying, I don't want to know it.

MISS VIOLET: You joke around. That's no good. Life is too short for jokes. (*Jim comes.*)

JIM: You know the hen who lays the golden eggs?

FRL. EMMA: I'm sure there are a lot. It's just unfortunate I haven't met one yet.

JIM: So stupid! I search and search, and I find nothing. And nothing again. Everything is a strain. The hen that lays the golden egg, according to my father, is capital. Where am I going to find capital, I wonder. Houses, properties. That's it I think, and I go for it. And the result? I barely make it. And Saturdays I treat myself: two broads! One of you is going to stay out in the cold and freeze. That's how it is and it doesn't bother me. (*Roma B. suffers a coughing fit. She coughs and coughs.*) The clever disqualify themselves. Only the dumb are unaware of their limits. (*Jim goes off with Miss Violet and Frl. Emma von Waldenstein.*)

ROMA B.: (*Coughing hard.*) Happiness is not always fun. (*The Rich Jew, the Little Prince and the Dwarf enter.*)

RICH JEW: Last testament from the emphysema ward.

LITTLE PRINCE: That's Roma B., boss, she's constantly freezing.

RICH JEW: Cities are cold and it's only fitting that people freeze there. Why do they build themselves such cities?

DWARF: (*Suffers a fit of laughing.*)

RICH JEW: If he doesn't stop laughing, I'll kick him out.

LITTLE PRINCE: If you don't stop laughing, gnome, he'll kick you out.

DWARF: The Rich Jew when he laughs can chase the Christian straight to hell.

RICH JEW: I'm not a Jew the way Jews are Jews. If you didn't know . . . The Little Prince, Madame. If he behaves himself he will inherit everything I own. Just between us, I often smile when I think of death. What else can we do? Good behavior is nothing to be ashamed of. Right?

LITTLE PRINCE: Certainly, sir. Good behavior is nothing to be ashamed of.

RICH JEW: Yes, yes. And this dwarf, this monster, the gnome: I feed him when I'm in a good mood. Which unfortunately, is quite often, because business is good, Madame, I can't complain. Give her a handkerchief, dwarf, so she can wipe the slime off her puss. (*The Dwarf goes to Roma B. Wipes her face.*)

DWARF: He builds houses, you know, and tears down the old ones. That makes him rich. And unpleasant too, you should know. But then he's not happy; it makes him easier to take.

RICH JEW: Does he know if people like us are happy? How could he know that?

LITTLE PRINCE: He doesn't know anything, boss. He gabs because that's what gabbers do: gab. Who listens to dwarves?

RICH JEW: Who knows—the fact that no one knows who trusts them makes them dangerous. Luckily there are very few of them.

DWARF: There have long been too many of your type.

RICH JEW: He's just saying that without thinking. The plump whore, by the way, disappointed me. She wasn't worth the asking price. For that matter— who is?

LITTLE PRINCE: He sent her away and didn't touch her. That means something. He says he's potent. And he refused.

RICH JEW: She talks like a waterfall and thinks I am an airhead because I need a whore. What's that supposed to mean? A whore needs the man who pays her. The man the whore. The simplest business in the world. And the most honest. Have you asked Madame if she can spare a tiny little hour for a rich Jew? I think she can indeed even if my dick is circumcised. It's more hygenic. Explain that to her, in case she doesn't already know from experience. (*Roma B. gets up, the Dwarf helps her.*)

DWARF: He's disgusting, young lady, but he pays well. And his potency, his fabled potency is a fairy tale. Nothing to be afraid of.

RICH JEW: OK, gang. You can crawl into your beds and wear out your foreskins. Alright, get on it. Beat it. (*He shoos them off the stage.*) Am I a Jew who must extract revenge on little people?! That's how it should be, and it's fitting. And peace and quiet, Madame, is amazingly gratifying. You don't have to respond. Thank you. I'm sick of conversations inflated with lies that do nothing but waste time, which all of us could put to better use. This image is enchantingly beautiful, the city which devotes itself to ruin. So—come. Your diseased lungs should pay off for you.

(*They leave. The stage grows dark. Marie Antoinette stands in a spotlight. She sings the "Song of the City."*)

MARIE ANTOINETTE:
To her they refused any sort of reply
Nor had they the answer required

She lived her life lonely, didn't ask why
And sold herself stripped of desire

She spread her legs open for armies of men
But never a one did she love
What had she learned for herself: it was hate, my friend
Whose feeling's a gift from above.

It was just yesterday she shaved herself clean
And laughed in despair all the while
Her shame would be deep if her mother had seen
And she thinks: could death be so vile.

A meaningless thing is your life
It's meaningless too if you're dead
God: he's bequeathed you the knife,
And th' blood of your enemy's red

Her father quite often screwed her with pleasure
She laughed at it, proud of her lot
Then he went away, left her to her leisure
And she forgave him—so what.

Often beat to a pulp by her mother
Because of her father's quick flight
She'd dream she was rich like some others
Possessed by this dream as her right

She hired a killer to beat mother dead
Then joyfully laughed loud and clear
And day after day still hanging her head
Knows why as a whore she stands her.

A meaningless thing is your life, *etc.* . . . .

(*Afterwards the stage is empty, as the light goes on again. Roma B. and the Rich Jew enter.*)

## Scene 4

RICH JEW: Do you know that sometimes I'm afraid? You don't know nor why. Business is going too well, which is asking for trouble. That plainly yearns to be punished. But instead of *it* receiving the punishment, fear punishes the frightened one—me. Me: nothing more than me. No freedom, no desire. To me you are beautiful. But it makes no difference. You could be however you liked. Beauty, for whom is that enough? I buy old houses in this city, tear them down, build new ones and they move well. The city protects me, it has to. Besides I'm a Jew. The police chief is my friend, in the broad sense of a friend; the mayor invites me over. I can count on the city council. No one particularly likes what he condones, but it's not my plan, it was there before I came. I have to be indifferent if children cry, if the old and the feeble suffer. I must be indifferent. And when some people scream in a rage I quite simply ignore it. What should I do otherwise? Burden my hunched back with a bad conscience? Develop sores? Suffer the plague? I believe in God, but in justice between four walls? Should my soul stand erect for the decisions of others that I only carry out with the profit which I need in order to get what I need? What do I need? Need, need—odd, when you repeat a word very often it loses its meaning, which it only possesses arbitrarily anyway. The city needs the unscrupulous businessman who allows it to transform itself. It must protect him thank you very much. After all, is it fear if you ask for the protection even before any danger signals appear? And fear—of gout. I smoke too much and nearly every day I read about these horrible things. Oh—forgive me, the hour is up. Three minutes overtime. That's going to cost you a pile of money, Jew. . . (*Hellfritz, Tenor and Achfeld carry a coffin across the stage. The realistic apartment kitchen is reconstructed. The Rich Jew and Roma B. exit dancing a minuet to the song of the two men.*)

HELLFRITZ, TENOR & ACHFELD:
The Itsy Bitsy Spider danced up the water spout;
Down came the rain and washed the spider out,
Up came the sun and dried up all the rain,
And the Itsy Bitsy Spider danced up the spout again.

### Scene 5

(*Franz B. is sitting in the room. Roma B. comes crashing in.*)

ROMA B.: Franz, Franz, look. Franz! Money. You can gamble. You can be some-body again with the others. They can't despise you anymore. No one's bet-ter than you, you're the greatest. Oh, Franz!

FRANZ B.: A grand. Is it true? A grand? In this cold? What did you do for it? Open your yap, whore, what did you do for the money?

ROMA B.: Nothing Franz. Nothing! You're hurting me. You're breaking my arm, Franz, be careful.

FRANZ B.: What did you do for the money? A grand in this cold. Did you lick his ass, you sow, you whore, did you lick his ass, eat his shit?! Open your mouth, shout the truth in my face before I kill you.

ROMA B.: I loved him. (*He throws her on the floor.*)

FRANZ B.: Whaaat? You loved him? You're the lowliest most disgusting pig I know. She loved him. What sort was he? Son of a millionaire? Tennis player? Love that kind of thing. I spit on this money. I spit on it.

ROMA B.: It's a Jew. A fat, ugly Jew. Not one of the ones you hate, Franz, not a tennis player. Just a Jew.

FRANZ B.: And? What did he do with you? Did he hit you? Step all over you? or . what else was it that was worth so much money?

ROMA B.: Nothing but love.

FRANZ B.: Did he pay that much because his cock is so big? Did he stretch your cunt, make your hole into a cavern? Did you scream with pleasure? Was it fun? Talk!

ROMA B.: His cock is very big.

FRANZ B.: Yeah finally. How big?

ROMA B.: Maybe twenty centimeters. Probably bigger.

FRANZ B.: Probably bigger! You filthy pig. And what else?

ROMA B.: It's thick. Very thick.

FRANZ B.: How thick?

ROMA B.: Like a beer bottle. Probably even thicker.

FRANZ B.: She let herself get fucked by a beer bottle. Broads! One like the next. All the same. And what else?

ROMA B.: He has endurance. He lasted a good hour. (*Franz B. grabs her and gives her a long kiss. Then he runs out. Roma B. sinks to the floor and coughs. Frl. Tau comes in.*)

FRL. TAU: I was just walking by outside and heard you. You ought to go in, I thought, maybe you can help.

ROMA B.: Thanks. But nothing can help me. It's very nice of you, anyway.

FRL. TAU: I just heard the cough, it was you for sure. You have to take care of yourself, health comes first.

ROMA B.: What are you talking about, woman? And who to?

FRL. TAU: My God, a body's constantly in the crap, what you're asked to do just to find a little niche for yourself. Sometimes I hardly even know who it is that's talking. It just burbles right out of me. You'll have to forgive me.

ROMA B.: There's nothing at all to forgive. You mean well. Although—that's perhaps the worst thing. When someone means well by another. I feel lousy. It's the cold, you know. And the stones. You can leave.

FRL. TAU: I don't like to be a bother.

ROMA B.: Hardly anyone does. There are a lot of bad ones. But usually evil has a method, right. And it almost always pursues a goal.

FRL. TAU: This won't be your path to salvation.

ROMA B.: Who wants to save herself? And from what? Who even knows herself?

FRL. TAU: Good evening. (*Frl. Tau leaves. Light change. Kraus, Peter stands in a spotlight. He lip syncs with a record.*)

KRAUS, PETER: "I'm just a lonely teenager . . ." (*Frl. Emma von Waldenstein, Asbach-Lilly, Miss Violet, Marie-Antoinette, Hellfritz, Tenor, and Jim form the ballet. Roma B. lies on the floor groaning. She makes love to Kraus, Peter. Platonically, it goes without saying. By the end of the song just Roma B. as well as*

*Herr and Frau Müller on stage. Herr Müller prepares himself for his daily appearance as a transvestite. Frau Muller sits in a wheelchair.)*

## Scene 6

MULLER: She's your daughter, Luise.

FRAU MULLER: Because she wasn't your son.

MULLER: Can't kill yourself.

FRAU MULLER: She's still living.

MULLER: Too bad. To that I can only repeat: too bad.

FRAU MULLER: Please take a look at yourself. You're running around like a tiger, completely riled.

MULLER: What's supposed to calm me down? This house maybe? Where every other minute someone is doing himself in?

FRAU MULLER: You're exaggerating.

MULLER: The correct degree of exaggeration is the closest one gets to a precise formulation.

FRAU MULLER: You're bluffing.

MULLER: If you say so.

FRAU MULLER: It's love. Someone ditched her.

MULLER: You don't get ditched in this day and age. At thirteen years old! That seems slightly exaggerated to me.

FRAU MULLER: Now eat.

MULLER: How am I supposed to eat with a crazy daughter in the house?

FRAU MULLER: She's not crazy. She's sick.

MULLER: Same thing.

FRAU MULLER: You'd sell yourself for a joke, even a lousy one.

MULLER: Look, I'm already selling myself for much less.

FRAU MULLER: You said it.

MULLER: If it's *too little* for you, please . . . I won't stand in your way. But take your daughter along, please. Should you forget her, I'll toss her out the window.

FRAU MULLER: You're brutal, and you leap from one extreme to another.

MULLER: She was already masturbating as a two year old.

FRAU MULLER: That's normal.

MULLER: God knows at that age I wasn't masturbating.

FRAU MULLER: You're just a late developer.

MULLER: I have long ago reconciled myself to having become a laughing stock to the people of this earth.

FRAU MULLER: You really ought to sing sentences like that, instead of just uttering them.

MULLER: Lord, at least I have my nights.

FRAU MULLER: Don't forget your lunchpail again.

MULLER: Lend me your dark red lipstick, would you honey. I seem to have lost mine.

FRAU MULLER: You should take better care of your things. The money's getting short.

MULLER: My God! Is there a human being on this earth who could stand this relentless carping?

FRAU MULLER: No one's carping. I'm only talking.

MULLER: You despise me. I can tell you that right now.

FRAU MULLER: You say that to me every day. And still I don't despise you.

MULLER: Who is it for God's sake who ditched her?

FRAU MULLER: A Yugoslav, I think. Some foreigner, anyway.

MULLER: Listen to that! A Yugoslav ditches my daughter, and goes unpunished.

FRAU MULLER: I guess he didn't love her.

MULLER: That's just how it's got to be. Because she doesn't eat and she's too skinny. But it's your fault too, Luise. Because you spoil her at every opportunity.

FRAU MULLER: If it makes things easier for you, I'll bear whatever guilt you want, and ask God's forgiveness.

MULLER: You're joking. That's not fitting for a mother. Be a dear and fetch me a pair of nylons from the bedroom. Tonight I'll wear the ones with seams. They're on the left. Or in the night stand. I hid them away because I'm afraid of your daughter. She steals, I tell you.

FRAU MULLER: Roma doesn't steal, Roma borrows.

MULLER: Borrows, and then returns them with runs. That's worse than theft. That's . . . the word escapes me. I'm sorry.

FRAU MULLER: Whatever word escaped you, honey, it's the wrong one.

MULLER: So what. Help me into my dress, please. Thanks. Now. How do I look?

FRAU MULLER: Enchanting, honest. As ever.

MULLER: Really?

FRAU MULLER: Really, really, honey. You know I don't lie.

MULLER: (Sings.) "Why shouldn't a woman have an affair, have an affair. Is she pretty, they will say"—is she asleep?

FRAU MULLER: Yes. She's asleep.

MULLER: And I can't see her?

FRAU MULLER: No, maybe another time.

MULLER: Thanks. Have you ordered the taxi, Luise?

FRAU MULLER: Yes. It should be here any minute. (*Herr and Frau Müller exit. A tango follows, danced by Roma B. and Marie-Antoinette. A breath of cold eroticism.*)

## Scene 7

(*Kitchen. Enter Franz.*)

FRANZ B.: It's tough, I tell you.

ROMA B.: You lost all of it, right?

FRANZ B.: Easy come easy go.

ROMA B.: So be it.

FRANZ B.: And the horses weren't running the way I handicapped them. That's fate.

ROMA B.: That's not fate—that's stupidity.

FRANZ B.: You say it like you know it. But it makes no difference.

ROMA B.: Thanks.

FRANZ B.: You feeling bad?

ROMA B.: How do you mean?

FRANZ B.: You seem so different today. So—superior. But sad to say I'm not pissed at you any more.

ROMA B.: It's hard to breathe. That's all.

FRANZ B.: You, your kind, pissing and moaning. Nothing else occurs to you.

ROMA B: I'm not complaining, Franz. That's not my way. I am merely stating a fact.

FRANZ B.: Listening to you like this, a person could easily take you for rational.

ROMA B.: And would be wrong, I know.

FRANZ B.: Come here—I want to give you a rub. That's right, good girl. You are my good little girl. You are, aren't you? (*A knock.*)

FRANZ B.: Yes! (*Frl. Emma von Waldenstein enters.*)

FRL. EMMA: Excuse me, am I disturbing you?

FRANZ B.: You can see that for yourself. But it makes no difference. We're in no hurry.

FRL. EMMA: It's on account of the sugar. You had promised to lend me some, Roma. Because today's Saturday, you know.

FRANZ B.: Oh! What theatre!

ROMA B.: Come in, Emma. I'll give you the sugar. Just come on in. (*Franz B. opens a beer. The two women go out, whispering to each other. Then the Little Prince stands in the door.*)

LITTLE PRINCE: Is this Fräulein B's place?

FRANZ B.: It's my place.

LITTLE PRINCE: But—there's a B on the door.

FRANZ B.: Then why do you ask?

LITTLE PRINCE: That's right. It was indeed rather superfluous.

FRANZ B.: Rather. Sure enough.

LITTLE PRINCE: That's my way, you know. I enjoy expressing myself a trifle affectedly. It was easy to learn, and has a great effect. And then, my boss, the Rich Jew, values this . . .

FRANZ B.: Who?

LITTLE PRINCE: The Rich Jew. Surely you've heard of him.

FRANZ B.: Out!

LITTLE PRINCE: Oh, you needn't take it so tragically. I think it's only a mood. And there are some who can afford to have moods.

FRANZ B.: Come here a second.

LITTLE PRINCE: Yes?

FRANZ B.: Is it true that his cock is as big and thick as a bottle?

LITTLE PRINCE: I can't say for sure. I only saw it once, when he was pissing. Because—even Jews have to piss. And what I saw then was rather less impressive.

FRANZ B.: Rather less.

LITTLE PRINCE: But—as you well know, amazing things can happen with cocks. Oh dear. The lady isn't perchance here?

FRANZ B.: Perchance rather less. But she's here.

LITTLE PRINCE: So.

FRANZ B.: Yes.

LITTLE PRINCE: Aha. Oh dear I really don't want to be impolite, but I would very much like to speak to her.

FRANZ B.: Does he want to (gesture) her again?

LITTLE PRINCE: He's a rather reticent human being. Even his closest friends rarely know for sure what he's planning.

FRANZ B.: Rather reticent. Roma!!! (Roma comes in.)

ROMA B.: Oh, I'm not ready.

LITTLE PRINCE: Makes no difference. He expects you the way you are. Come.

(Franz B. sips at his beer and is pretty astonished that he is alone all of a sudden. Oscar von Leiden is in the room.)

OSCAR VON LEIDEN: I wanted to talk to Fräulein B. I must excuse myself.

FRANZ B.: She's at the Jew's, where she gets paid.

OSCAR VON LEIDEN: Yes, I heard he was spending time with her. That's why I'm here. I've done her an injustice. After all, I couldn't guess that she'd have this kind of status, overnight, so to speak.

FRANZ B.: Status?

OSCAR VON LEIDEN: Indeed. As of today this address is highly valued among the better circles.

FRANZ B.: What are you saying?

OSCAR VON LEIDEN: Personally I am less interested in women, I can gladly tell you that. But one does what one can.

FRANZ B.: Are you—I mean to say, of the other persuasion? Hmmm?

OSCAR VON LEIDEN: I'm selective. On the one hand I do what I enjoy. On the other, what's necessary to keep myself from being talked about. My father has business dealings with the Jew, and the Jew with him. They chase each others's shadows.

FRANZ B.: I've never tried it.

OSCAR VON LEIDEN: Chasing your shadow?

FRANZ B.: The other thing. What you enjoy.

OSCAR VON LEIDEN: Doesn't cost you anything. Give it a try.

FRANZ B.: Would you . . . have anything against helping me . . . try it.

OSCAR VON LEIDEN: I'm not very choosy. And life is shorter than it has a right
to be.

## Scene 8

(*Light change. Herr Müller stands in the spotlight and sings: "That Won't Make the
World Go Under." When the lights return we are in a club. Only a few patrons.
Roma B. and the Rich Jew.*)

RICH JEW: This man is your father, correct? It wasn't difficult to find that out.
He visited you now and again as a customer, am I not right? Stay, sit down.
I'm no prude. On the contrary. It lends you a somewhat morbid charm. You
should cash in on that. You know, I make everything pay off for me. Each
and every fart, if you will allow me a trite phrase. You should take my advice. I go through this city as if it weren't chaotic, uninhabitable like the
moon, as though it were open, honest, straight up and down. And I laugh
all the while, grinning 'til my teeth grind to stubs. Müller! I'll present your
father to you, take it calmly. I wanted to introduce you, Müller—Fräulein B.
Two darling people. By the way, you were wonderful again today.

MULLER: Yes? Thank you. On some days one makes a special effort.

RICH JEW: Quite right, quite right. And you know why you do, wouldn't you
say?

MULLER: Yes, one knows why. So it is written.

RICH JEW: And the Mrs.? Is she well?

MULLER: Reading Lenin same as ever. And Marx.

RICH JEW: There have surely been worse bodies of wisdom, as you know.

MULLER: As I know.

RICH JEW: Yes, yes—one is never too old to learn. And new experiences always
replace the old. When necessary, enemies become friends. Days wane and
make room for new days. He who knows how to help himself, helps himself,
and so forth. Am I right?

MULLER: As always.

RICH JEW: Thank you. You can go. And have a drink on me. Even two, if your
health permits. Goodbye.

MULLER: Goodbye. Good evening, dear lady.

ROMA B.: Good evening.

RICH JEW: A charming fellow, don't you think? One could almost forget that his name is Müller.

(*The light changes. Marie-Antoinette and Jim stand in the light. They sing a duet from* La Traviata. *They are naked. Then the curtain descends. It is time for Intermission.*)

# PART TWO

## Scene 9

*(Roma B.'s apartment. Dusk.)*

ROMA B.: Instead of being happy and letting the sun shine on your belly you crawl back into yourself and search for something you'll never find.

FRANZ B.: I'm afraid, Roma, and it makes me shake.

ROMA B.: What frightens you? And what causes you to shake?

FRANZ B.: The dimensions of the whole thing. You establish bank accounts, buy houses, drive cars into the ground without batting an eyelash. A half year ago we didn't have money to pay the grocer. It's growing and growing, getting out of hand.

ROMA B.: You don't love me anymore.

FRANZ B.: No. I don't love you anymore. I loved you in the crap, the filth. My feelings can't quite cut it in the high life.

ROMA B.: That's a paradox.

FRANZ B.: Maybe you're right. But why you? Why should they want to make *you* rich? What do you have that they need?

ROMA B.: Don't ask questions, Franz. The answers could be frightening.

FRANZ B.: I'll pack my bag and go into the city which will swallow me up as it has swallowed many before me.

ROMA B.: There are rumors.

FRANZ B.: There always are.

ROMA B.: You are supposed to have changed, they say, supposed to be different from what you were.

FRANZ B.: What's your opinion?

ROMA B.: I have no opinion. I'm in love.

FRANZ B.: Yes. With me. And for that I'm sorry. But I can't change it.

ROMA B.: I'll give you money. The way you tear yourself apart shouldn't go unrewarded. And I needed you so very much, Franz. I had nothing but you , and your fists, which kept me awake.

FRANZ B.: Don't be sad, Roma. Everything comes to an end, that's in the nature of things.

ROMA B.: Do you love this . . . other person?

FRANZ B.: Love—? Roma. What can I tell you.

ROMA B.: Never the truth, that's for sure. Truth hurts, and lies help us to survive.

FRANZ B.: I'll never forget you, my little one. Your skinny little arms, your frightened eyes. But I can't do otherwise. And this fear of things which my brain can't comprehend. My temples are throbbing and throbbing. And my blood roars and stops up my ears.

ROMA B.: Yes. You must go, that I understand. (*He gives her one more tender caress. As he leaves, Jim comes across the stage.*)

JIM: (*Sings.*) I'm just a journeyman traveler, good night, dear lady, good night. Quite thin is my jerkin, quite thick is my fur, good night, dear lady, good night.

DWARF: Spiders! Lots of little black spiders. The city is groaning under the spiders. It's trembling and moaning. The spiders are becoming a plague. They will be a plague until the city has learned to derive pleasure from them. Spiders!

## Scene 10

(*Hans von Gluck and Roma B.*)

HANS VON GLUCK: He's sucking us dry, the Jew. Drinking our blood and blaming everything on us because he's a Jew and we're guilty. I rack my brains and I brood. I tear at my nerves. I'm going under. I wake up nights, my throat like it's in a noose, death stalking me in person. My reason tells me they're just images, myths from the pre-history of our fathers. I feel a sharp pain on my left side. My heart, I ask myself? Or the gallbladder? And it's the Jew's fault. Just being there he makes us guilty. If he stayed where he came from or if they gassed him I'd be able to sleep better. They forgot to gas him. This is no joking matter. And I rub my hands together as I imagine him breathing his last in the gas chamber. I rub my hands together again and I moan and I rub and I say "I'm Rumpelstiltskin: ah how fine that no one knows this name is mine." He's always one step ahead and all he leaves us is charity. Garbage, worthless objects. Something in me whispers, "your hour is up," and for the hundreth time I clutch my heart and curse this system that bleeds me. Which makes me sick, right here where it finds me. Is it possible to run for it with a suitcase full of real estate? You get tempted by Siren songs—the houses, the property—and you're back so you can be tortured again and bleeding. And someone exists who is laughing up his sleeve all the while, and he's bought you out even before you've thought of selling. He has the banks and city hall on his side. You give up, and in the next minute you're tightening your grip on the same property which is causing you the pain. The doctors lie to your face, they're all bedfellows, they keep you alive until you've suffered enough, and 'til the gods, whoever they are, have been able to jerk off while watching you suffer. The gods hate you, and they need you to satisfy their perverse desires. They're nothing but witches and fairies, the stuff of children's nightmares, invented to prepare you for life—which is death. The Jew knows his business well, fear's a stranger to him, he's not frightened by death, him. He doesn't have a life to live. I know, my time's up. I've had the honorarium transferred to your account. My heartfelt thanks.

## Scene 11

*(While the leather bar is being set up, a loud tape: "Play Habanero One More Time For Me" by Caterina Valente. The whole cast is in the leather bar. Most of those present wear leather costumes with medals and other such nonsense. Marie-Antoinette is waiting for her entrance. Muller is in a gaudy dress.)*

RICH JEW: I am gradually withdrawing from business life. The night has taken me captive with its sweet vices, as the big city, the metropolis has created them.
DWARF: The businesses are getting out of hand. He's lying in his own best interest.
RICH JEW: He's learned quite well to be the antagonist, the dwarf. Still, he's never completely convincing.
LITTLE PRINCE: He's allowed too many liberties. He runs out of steam too quickly.
RICH JEW: Because he's so little. But we can be certain he won't grow anymore. Müller! At home precisely wherever the city redeems itself in novelty and degeneracy.
MULLER: Life doesn't exactly give you free choice. The city demands its tribute.
RICH JEW: Which, what's more, some willingly pay. I know that for a fact, I know my way around.
MARIE ANTOINETTE: (Sings.)
My leatherboy.

Leatherboy
All out of leather
Same as the rest
Yes, by the way, friend,
You're one like the next.
Does it protect souls
This uniform?
For when I beat you
It's pleasure you groan.
Man—yes, what is that?
No need to fear
Pissing their beds wet
Combing their hair.
Call up your mommy
Be not afraid
Eat your salami
You've got it made
That hair on your chest
It's only for show
Scream out in lust
To sleep will I go
Drink up your milk, guy
Let heave with a moan
Then after a good cry,
Come on back home.
All out of leather
Same as the rest
Yes, by the way, friend,
You're one like the next.

(*A ruckus erupts out of the applause.*)

RICH JEW: Life at last!
ROMA B.: Franz!
RICH JEW: Sit down! Quick! You have your duty to perform.
MULLER II: Men don't kiss men here, sir.
KRAUS, PETER: Take off his pants, the pig. He wants it that way.
ACHFELD: Castrate the jerk! We'll slice his balls right out of their sack!
HELLFRITZ, TENOR: I'll hold him. Let's go.

(*Two of them hold Franz B. The others undress him. They have their chains and whips ready. When Franz B. is naked, they start to hit him. Frl. Emma von Waldenstein holds a bucket of water and the others repeatedly dunk Franz B.'s head into it.*)

*Oscar von Leiden prays the "Our Father."*)

FRANZ B.: This is insanity!

KRAUS, PETER: Pain, pal!

MULLER II: The way you love it!

FRANZ B.: Paradise!

ACHFELD: His balls! Rip them out.

FRANZ B.: You do love me! My God, you do love me.

KRAUS, PETER: Like a bitch.

MULLER: What's the story with the whore? Does she love you?

FRANZ B.: She does love me!

ACHFELD: And you?

FRANZ B.: I love you! Shove your fist up my ass, tear me apart, let me hear the angels singing.

JIM: Now into the water with the pig!

FRANZ B.: Do me good. Destroy me!

ACHFELD: Rip out his balls.

FRANZ B.: Burn me, shove nails through my nipples. I want to bleed.

MULLER II: You'll never be as you were again.

FRANZ B.: The ego is other. Fists, friends! Take me gently. That's good. Fists up my ass 'til I die.

HELLFRITZ, TENOR: Careful, he musn't be killed.

FRANZ B.: Thanks! I thank you. Degrade me again and again. Let me discover humility. (*They let him fall like a wet sack, and leave the club.*)

MULLER: (*Sings.*) "I just wanna be loved by you." (*Müller uses his wig to wipe the blood off Franz B. Marie Antoinette sings: "Sleep little baby sleep, your father's a . . ."*)

RICH JEW: So the city redeems itself in its forgiving gestures. It all evens out in the end, all the same.

DWARF: It's a game. The rules are set up, the victor identified—before the game even begins.

RICH JEW: So what? The unfathomable doesn't take anyone in anymore. We're totally booked 'til the end of the century.

LITTLE PRINCE: Who knows his text sings his songs, the silent roles scare the children.

RICH JEW: And the man who wants to get paid on Friday builds houses with his hands. Beyond that he's not worth talking about.

DWARF: The beast has contempt for the sweat on beauty's brow. The contempt earns him money and a peaceful night's sleep—with a clear conscience.

RICH JEW: It's your role. You've learned it without paying attention to the cue. Now you babble away the right words in the wrong place and have no effect. I am submerging myself in culture and exotic atmosphere. I'm beginning to forget the value of money. I had a goal. It has become relative. Nevertheless it continues. I set it in motion, now it must run its course.

LITTLE PRINCE: And don't forget us, who are here for your sake, at your service, to realize ideas which are worth realizing. Your fee, dear lady, has been paid directly into your account. You'll be pleased. Good night. (*The Rich Jew, the Dwarf and the Little Prince leave.*)

FRL. EMMA: The city no longer guarantees equal opportunity.

ROMA B.: It never has.

ASBACH-LILLY: But the discrepancies were never as shocking as now.

ROMA B.: Should I pass up opportunities that come my way? Who in the world would do that?

FRL. TAU: Everyone. Not like you. We wouldn't make the others feel inferior.

ROMA B.: I'm just looking after my own interests.

FRL. EMMA: But with what arrogance, what grace. It's the grace that comes with contempt.

ROMA B.: I feel contempt for no one anymore. I've even stopped despising men.

MISS VIOLET: That's it. She doesn't despise men anymore. Have you forgotten the rules of the game—to despise the man who pays for love.

ROMA B.: There is no love where there's contempt.

FRL EMMA: Not true. It's only where there's contempt love has a right to exist.

ROMA B.: But then the world would be full of love. Why isn't it?

ASBACH-LILLY: Because people always upset the balance, think more of themselves than the whole.

ROMA B.: Well, what is the whole? The power inside me is my whole. The whole is illusory.

FRL. EMMA: We're getting lost in discussion when we've long been of the same opinion.

ROMA B.: I'm taking nothing from anyone. I live for myself and I'm trying to find an  answer in myself.

FRL TAU: You're robbing us of our ability to be happy. You're showing us limits which we don't want to see, which we wouldn't have to see if they weren't the way they are.

MISS VIOLET: You're working against your own sex.

ASBACH-LILLY: You are man's brother, an enemy of your sister.

FRL. EMMA: In future we have nothing in common. To us you're on the other side. Now you are alone. See how you manage. (*The whores leave.*)

ROMA B.: How's he doing?

MULLER: He'll live.

ROMA B.: But does he want to?

MULLER: Only those with the power to apprehend souls know that. (*A short pause.*)

ROMA B.: What's it mean—the Jew using me to fight you?

MULLER: He raises you up to humiliate me. The idea is simple.

ROMA B.: Have you caused him so much suffering?

MULLER: He thinks I'm to blame for the death of his parents.

ROMA B.: And? Is it true?

MULLER: I wasn't concerned with each and every one of the people I murdered. I wasn't an individualist. I am a technocrat. But it's possible I am his parents' murderer, I'd be glad of it. And I am glad of it.

ROMA B.: The burden is yours, and it makes you happy.

MULLER: It's no burden to be a Jew killer when you have convictions like mine.

ROMA B.: And the degradation doesn't affect you?

MULLER: It's not really meant for me, but it does set you to thinking what kind of country this is which permits the kinds of thing which occur here every-day.

ROMA B.: Times have changed.

MULLER: Not really. At bottom everything's the way it was, and has its own good order. What more can a person do than wait? So I'm waiting 'til my rights are rights again.

ROMA B.: You have a lot of time, father.

MULLER: Centuries, Roma. We won't die out, and each new face of suffering heaped on us makes us freer and strong. Fascism will be victorious.

ROMA B.: I'm ok. I can afford the life I want to live.

MULLER: So you should, Roma. Don't develop scruples for your father's sake. Father will save you. Father's on the right side.

JIM: (Sings.) "A soldier stands on the bank of the Volga . . . " (Frau Müller enters in a wheelchair.)

FRAU MULLER: Come home. It's so quiet without you.

MULLER: I'm coming. This is your daughter. Do you still recognize her?

FRAU MULLER: She has grown thin.

MULLER: She was always thin, but things are going well for her. She's rich.

FRAU MULLER: That makes it easier for me to hate her.

ROMA B.: Why does my mother hate her child?

MULLER: Because you're young and beautiful, and you have legs, Roma, which carry you. Hers fail her. Basically, she hates herself.

FRAU MULLER: You talk and talk, and think you know it all. And you conjure up images which don't connect with reality. And yet I won't despair, I'll fight for our happiness. We won't allow ourselves to be eaten alive by the hardships others invent for us to suffer under them. (Herr Müller rolls his wife offstage. Roma B. quite alone. Franz B. still lies unconscious on the floor. A Gregorian Chorale from the tape recorder, the stage is a cathedral. Oscar von Leiden still praying.)

ROMA B.: This is not a life worth living. God! Puke, and afterward you feel better. But us? We hate each other, fight amongst ourselves, instead of show-ing solidarity. And that's the way you willed it, God! Give mankind understanding, but not the wherewithall to fulfill its promise. We are burning, and you fix your gouty finger on us. All that I have endured, the pain, the relentless desires of the multitude. What am I? Your deputy on earth? A thing which makes the city worth living in? But just a thing, not human. Something to dump on, fruitless sperm and pain and sorrow. And the city turns us into living corpses, horror figures without an adequate chamber, subway people with streets which poison us, where we can be poisoned some more. With pain which frightens us when things are going too well. And each pleasure conceals deadly remorse within itself, and only the murderers save themselves because their lives have meaning. That at least they've done their best. I see no further reason to endure those things that kill me without really killing me. I kiss the dead, taste the taste of the long deceased, decay will be my hymn book, disgust my pleasure. And I'd sing songs which defy the abyss, I'd be a beast who grubbed for monkey brains, live ones. But I don't do it, I let myself get swallowed up. You have to be what's required of you, otherwise you're lost thoroughly, down and out. God, I no longer want to live this life. I want to give it away, sacrifice myself to the city which needs its victims in order to appear alive itself, and finally to save me, to save myself from living death which makes me the same as those who have forgotten what it is to live. Who've grown stupid, who can't even speak, and who imagine themselves happy and forget that they really aren't, and who don't grow teeth to assert themselves in the jungle. God, I retire. Clear off. I'll find someone to make me happy.

JIM: You are very lonely.

ROMA B.: That's not it.

JIM: But you are.

ROMA B.: Yes. I am lonely.

JIM: Look. We all are.

ROMA B.: Kill me.

JIM: I have no reason to kill.

ROMA B.: There's reason enough.

JIM: Maybe. But I sing. That takes enough effort. That's all. (Jim goes off. Kraus, Peter enters, wants to cross the stage.)

ROMA B.: Stop! Stand still!

KRAUS, PETER: I'm in a hurry.

ROMA B.: We all are.

KRAUS, PETER: What do you want then?

ROMA B.: To die.

KRAUS, PETER: My time is too valuable for this kind of luxury. Good day. (He leaves.)

ROMA B.: You're obsessed with yourself.

OSCAR VON LEIDEN: To yearn for death is so much easier than mastering life.

ROMA B.: You won't stop me.

OSCAR VON LEIDEN: Well who could. I love your husband.

ROMA B.: That's your affair.

OSCAR VON LEIDEN: You don't despise us.

ROMA B.: I haven't had the strength to despise anyone for quite some time.

OSCAR VON LEIDEN: You've been good for me. (*Oscar von Leiden picks Franz B. up from the stage and carries him off like Jesus his cross. Kraus, Peter, Jim, Hellfritz, Tenor, Müller II, Achfeld and Hans von Gluck cross the stage singing, "Oh You Beautiful Western Woods." The last to file by are the Rich Jew and the Little Prince. They remain.*)

RICH JEW: I noticed you need me.

ROMA B.: I failed.

RICH JEW: Don't talk.

ROMA B.: I renounce my role. It doesn't satisfy me.

RICH JEW: The show's over. Anyway you have already fulfilled your purpose.

ROMA B.: I've known that for some time. I forgave you.

RICH JEW: You have no right to forgive me. It's none of your concern.

ROMA B.: I know what's due me. I have no right to forgive, no right to demand. No rights at all. That's my only hope. Abject. Powerless. That's my only hope.

RICH JEW: We have never listened to music together, can you remember?

ROMA B.: I know my way around. Music could have deluded us.

RICH JEW: And who'd have had the need to be deluded?

ROMA B.: All of us. We need songs which sing of love.

RICH JEW: You are in despair. But your despair is worthless. You can't deal with this kind of despair.

ROMA B.: I didn't have business dealings in mind.

RICH JEW: If you are trying to hurt me you won't succeed.

ROMA B.: You know that best for yourself.

RICH JEW: I could forgive you if I wanted to.

ROMA B.: Yes. But I don't accept your forgiveness. You're no comfort to me.

RICH JEW: Are you so sure?

ROMA B.: No. Maybe you are right. Maybe once more it is you who I need.

RICH JEW: You have already thought things through.

ROMA B.: Yes. I want to die.

RICH JEW: That's the best solution. We agree there.

ROMA B.: But I don't have the strength to do it.

RICH JEW: How should you? Do you have plans?

ROMA B.: No. I only have me to rely on. How could a brain like mine make plans?

RICH JEW: That is correct. Anything else?

ROMA B.: Do you want to do it for me? You could even find it pleasurable. And then— it won't take very long.

RICH JEW: And as for the question—do I have a reason? What would you answer?

ROMA B.: I could say I know too much, now, as I speak. But even that wouldn't be enough for you.

RICH JEW: No. That wouldn't be enough for me. I'll do it for you.

ROMA B.: Thanks. I'm tired and now I'll go to find my peace. Both of us know it's not much but it's the only thing we can do. It is a practical desire. But for whom will desire be put to rest? Don't make me wait any longer. (*The Rich Jew takes his necktie and strangles Roma B. She asphixiates without a sound. The Rich Jew leaves. The Little Prince falls to his knees.*)

LITTLE PRINCE: Oh my God, I thank you. He has killed her, he has disqualified himself. It's clear he loved her. Whoever loves has blown his rights.

(*He runs away. Hellfritz, Tenor and Achfeld come with the coffin and lay Roma B. in it. Perhaps they hum a tune. During this the set changes into the office of the chief of police. It's a skyscraper, 16th floor. Through the half open blinds one has a view of the whole city.*)

MULLER II: Yeah, and she lived longer than one could have expected.

KRAUS, PETER: So it goes. The city gobbles up its children.

MULLER II: Right where it finds them. Quite right.

KRAUS, PETER: Clues?

MULLER II: Clues enough. But what's the point?

KRAUS, PETER: Exactly. Let's file it.

MULLER II: So it goes. Depressing.

KRAUS, PETER: More or less, you know?

MULLER II: More or less. Right. Who suffers? The victim?

KRAUS, PETER: Absolutely not.

MULLER II: You see how fast people can agree on something.

KRAUS, PETER: They can. You're right. It's not worth the trouble.

MULLER II: The whole story will go right down the drain.

KRAUS, PETER: Where it belongs. Am I right?

MULLER II: You are, my good man, you are. (*The Little Prince comes.*)

LITTLE PRINCE: It's my duty.

MULLER II: Everyone has to decide that for himself.

LITTLE PRINCE: That's how it is. And I've decided.

MULLER II: Then that surely is how it is.

LITTLE PRINCE: Yes. I know the murderer.

MULLER II: Which murderer? Are we looking for a murderer?

KRAUS, PETER: Not that I know of. No, we're not after a murderer.

MULLER II: Right. We are in fact not looking for a murderer.

LITTLE PRINCE: It may well be you're not looking for one, nevertheless you're going to find one, like it or not.

MULLER II: Why don't you leave the dead in peace? Have they been paid to let others make all this fuss about them? Even in hell to be forced to have their ears buzzing like this!

LITTLE PRINCE: This has to do with the living, and in this case with me. Namely: I will take over the business.

KRAUS, PETER: If anyone will listen to you.

LITTLE PRINCE: I'll know how to find the one to listen to me.

MULLER II: He seems resolute, wouldn't you say?

KRAUS, PETER: Yes. He seems rather determined.

MULLER II: Strange. Strange. That there's still one who doesn't know the laws of the city. What can a body do?

KRAUS, PETER: It's enough to make you despair.

LITTLE PRINCE: The Rich Jew killed her. They'll lock him up and throw away the key.

MULLER II: It is so sad. Why would someone give an answer when he hasn't been asked a question? But a man's private will is his divine right.

*(Kraus, Peter has snuck behind the Little Prince and whacked him on the head with a pistol. The Little Prince falls in a lump. Kraus, Peter picks him up and throws him out the window. He gazes after for a rather long time.)*

KRAUS, PETER: So! Such a pity. The things you have to do. It could easily spoil your whole life. *(Müller II picks up the telephone.)*

MULLER II: This is the Chief of Police, Müller II. Someone just leapt out of the window on me. Look after it, please. *(The Rich Jew and the Dwarf come.)*

RICH JEW: I was lucky. Someone almost fell on my head.

MULLER II: Yes, it was someone who no longer enjoyed life.

RICH JEW: Too bad, really. He was all-told an industrious little guy.

KRAUS, PETER: A little too industrious, that was it.

MULLER II: He knew about things which weren't his to know.

RICH JEW: I can imagine. These cities! What they turn us into. By the way the Dwarf here, this monster, can testify where I was when this murder occurred. A horrible affair, no?

DWARF: We were in the Western quarter at the time. Whatever time it has to be we were in the Western quarter doing business.

MULLER II: That's right my little one. He's a good boy, real good.

RICH JEW: If you're little you don't have much choice but to be a good boy, wouldn't you say?

DWARF: Yes indeed. *(Achfeld and Hellfritz, Tenor carry in Franz B. and throw him on the floor in front of Müller II.)*

MULLER II: You see—that's just the murderer we need to make things work out.

FRANZ B.: No!

MULLER II: You'll learn, pal, we'll be seeing eye to eye soon enough.

END

Denis Calandra is Professor of Theatre Emeritus, University of South Florida, Tampa. He has written for several professional and academic journals and is also the author of *New German Dramatists*.

Printed in the USA
CPSIA information can be obtained
at www.ICGtesting.com
JSHW021056071123
51599JS00004B/6